CW00468178

GREENWOOD DARK

Greenwood Dark

A Traveller's Poems

Christopher Somerville

HAUS PUBLISHING

LONDON

Copyright © 2008 Christopher Somerville

First published in Great Britain in 2008 by Haus Publishing Ltd,
26 Cadogan Court, Draycott Avenue, London SW3 3BX
www.hauspublishing.co.uk

The moral rights of the author have been asserted.

A CIP catalogue record for this book is available from the British Library

ISBN 978–1-905791–57–6

Designed and typeset in Garamond by MacGuru Ltd
info@macguru.org.uk

Printed in China by SC (Sang Choy) International Ltd.
Cover photograph courtesy Tim Shackleton
Frontispiece: *The Green Man* by Andrew Davidson

For my mother, Elizabeth Somerville, with love

Contents

* First published in *The Golden Step – A Walk through the Heart of Crete* by Christopher Somerville (Haus Publishing: 2007)

Introduction

THESE 100 POEMS were written between 1999 and 2008, and they form a journey: not so much a linear journey from A to B as a wandering exploration through the stories, landscapes, incidents and accidents, places and people I have encountered during worldwide travels over the past ten years.

Most poets avoid having to 'explain' their poems, on the grounds that poems are like magic boxes – they have many secret layers and compartments, most of which the poet himself has not yet discovered. But I have heard people say over and over again that they are put off reading and enjoying poems because poetry books simply present the poems on a 'take it or leave it' basis, with no contexts or keys. Here they are: if you don't get them, tough.

I hope that the way I have grouped these travel poems, and the notes that accompany each one, will encourage readers who have always thought of poetry as too obscure for them, while leaving mystery and magic intact in the poems.

GLIMPSES

As a travel writer I spend a lot of time in transport – trains, boats, planes, cars – staring out of the window. This is something that writers of poetry have always found fruitful, from Frances Cornford and her 'Fat Lady Seen From The Train' to Robert Louis Stevenson's 'From A Railway Carriage':

' ... here is a mill and there is a river:
Each a glimpse and gone for ever!'

The scene that is glimpsed momentarily and immediately snatched away seems loaded with significance. It stays in a corner of the mind, being slowly chewed over.

'SECRET SOWING' – I saw this figure from a train window as I raced between Bristol and London on a grey February day.

'GREENLAND BLUE' – A mesmerising glimpse looking down from a plane going between Britain and Canada, immediately after waking up from one of those troubled aeroplane dozes.

Secret sowing

I saw her turn her back in some
Berkshire field against a gale
slapping life into the pale
cheeks of day. Bright seeds
or pods gusted from her hand
over the closed face of the land.
The field ran and rose
to a black ridge of oak
and of transmitter masts that broke
into the shell of the sky. Energy
sparked and sucked: oaks blowing,
a wired sky and a secret sowing.

Greenland blue

I glanced out from a cloud to find Greenland
salted white with the bunched hide
of an old swimmer, semi-sunk
leviathan of a rich royal blue
stealing by, deep miles down.

Deadly blue ranges, mitigated by
such innocent snow; you pierced me on sight.

Call you greyland, or blackland:
the glimpse framed nothing easy, nothing
green or breathing. I must have trespassed some
high bright track of the gods to be
so struck with you, staring down between

Icarus wings over a waxen sea.
Greenland blue: I had not expected blue.

SKYWATCHING

Three events that lit up the skies in different ways:

'MIR FALLING' – The Russian space research station Mir was assembled in space over several missions that lasted ten years, from 1986–96. On 23 March 2001, maintenance funds having run out, Mir was removed from its orbit and steered to destruction in the Pacific Ocean. As the station re-entered the atmosphere it broke up in a dramatic display of fiery comet-like bodies. It seemed a spectacular but sad end to a bold venture.

'COMET SHOWER' – In November 1999 the northern sky was to be lit by a fabulous comet shower, well advertised in advance by the BBC. I was at the door of my Somerset cottage to witness it. But the night was cloudy and wet, and there wasn't a thing to be seen.

'SKYBOUND' – Walking up the slope of the Hog's Back in Surrey, I grumpily glared upwards as the snarling noise of a plane engine spoiled the peace of the day – then found myself transfixed by the beauty of the tiny stunt plane as it swooped audaciously about the sky.

Mir falling

Through salt, cold eyes
turn, swivel; some few million
receptors of momentary shocks to plankton
– who knows? – indifferently rise
to stars, to skies.

The breaking shoal,
fishlike and heavenly, crazes in its arc
from out there. Icarus ruins in spark
and brave splash of tail through the whole
almighty roll

downstream of sight.
Hearts slip seawards. The mission's done –
the impossible, all too human cast at the sun,
salmon jumps of the mind beyond night:
the dream of light.

One joyful leap
out of grasp, beauty raked across
what we called heaven: glorious loss.
Through salt, cold eyes stare at the short steep
slide to the deep.

Comet shower

Skywatchers tense, agog. Tonight
the brilliant spatter, a fall of young light:
punky graffiti splashed on the old
pocked face of night.
                November cold
slabs the doorway, and the seethe and mourn
of rain, sad curtain sulkily drawn
against such glory.
                So I'll tune blind eyes
into the clouds. Astronomers trawl skies
soberly, fastidious netsmen out to sift
what it is they want. Throw me the drift,
sight unseen, of how high born sparks
dance from God's anvil.
                His hammer arcs
playfully high, clouded out of ken;
celestial blacksmith, forging the script for when
the sky slides back and coruscating spaces
soundlessly race towards our upturned faces.

Skybound

I'll see you again one day as I
saw you then, rollercoastering
round in a blue twist of the sky.
You grabbed a hook from heaven and hauled straight
up there and hung at heaven's gate,
growling, and then went tumbling wing over wing
over the Hog's Back, teasing death
to whom you showed yourself for a breath.

Come for me, you joyful thing, some
day when I'm stiff clay and cannot wring
relish from anything; and when you come,
only touch the ground and we'll be found
roistering and rollercoastering,
in with all that's earthbound and skybound.

OTHER LIVES

HOWEVER GRACEFUL AN aeroplane, it can't begin to rival the aerial mastery of any bird. Watching a red kite maintaining its stance on the wind by infinitesimal, continuous adjustments of wings and tail, I can only admire such fitness for purpose. This specialised perfection also serves to highlight the vast, unbridgeable gulf of communication between humans and their fellow creatures.

'SWIFTS AND STARLINGS' was written at a table outside a café in the Sicilian mountain town of Enna. As the swifts circled in the summer dusk, I thought of the starlings that mass on winter evenings over the reedbeds of the Somerset Levels in huge, swirling congregations several million strong.

'FULMAR CIRCUIT' – The fulmar was circling just below the rim of the Antrim cliffs in Northern Ireland, near the magnificent and haunted ruin of Dunluce Castle. Two episodes in the castle's history had struck me. In 1584 its owner, Sorley Boy Macdonnell, had wrested the stronghold back from the English, who had taken it from him, by having his men hauled up the cliffs in baskets to attack the unsuspecting defenders. Half a century later, during a terrible storm in 1639, the kitchen wing collapsed into the sea with the loss of several lives.

'BLUE TIT ON A FENNEL HEAD' – The blue tit was in my mother's Somerset garden, where it allowed me to observe it from touching distance for as long as I wanted.

'MOUNTAINEER' AND 'DONKEY DAWN' both came about in May 1999 as I lazed for a fortnight in the mountain village of Thronos, a period of rest and recreation halfway through a 300-mile walk from end to end of Crete.

'PIG JOKE' – How tempting it is to anthropomorphise animals! A faceful of mud on a walk in the Thames country of Oxfordshire brought me right back down to earth.

'THE CRICKET' – It clung for a day to the back door of the light-house keeper's cottage at Start Point in South Devon, where I was on holiday. There was a sheer drop off the edge of the promontory to a secret beach far below, from where black-backed gulls would suddenly appear as if flung up out of the ground. I realised too late that the cottage garden was a prime hunting spot for raptors and gulls.

Swifts and starlings

Here with a *birra Moretti*, watching a fierce
old Sicilian get his grandson to spell
births and deaths from the paper, all feels well.
Swifts cut their saracen curves through the
sun-brazed sky: the coppery tang of a bell.

Oh to be in England on this perfect
eggshell-blue evening? Not while
Enna parades, young bucks make girls smile
out of their mothers' shadows, farmers creak
to Mass and boys rev bikes, man-style.

Still something pulls at my sleeve. It is
the thin steely screams of the swifts and their fast
circling over the town, a black cast
of metallic specks, calling to mind the starlings
as I saw them over Westhay Moor in the last

cold part of winter. Like iron filings
sucked by some magnet behind the Somerset sky;
like ropes to strangle men, a massed cry
that roared for mastery. Ten million, someone said.
They looked like that, an army sweeping by,

cramming the air, crushing trees to earth,
black fruit. Such unaccountable power.
And through them, like a man that knows his hour,
a faceless one drove a tractor, hunched
in a peaked hood. One from the dark tower,

lacking only the scythe. In this bright island
skeined and shadowed, where evenings fall
sharply and shutters close along the wall,
a balance strikes, bell-like: the rumpus and roar
of starlings, the swifts' blade of a call.

Fulmar circuit

Between sky and earth I watch the fulmar
turn again, plane by. The round
eye shiny as a blackberry bleb;

the circuit and circuit that may mean
something or nothing.
                        Those ounces of brain:
do they spark towards thought? What's

in the blank white face, in the
round eye, seeming to glance, that may not
even know me from sea pink and basalt?

Gulf wider than the plunge before Dunluce
stares between that eye and this.
Sorley Boy winching his baskets of men

up the walls of Antrim, the columnar cliffs
towards English screams and the casting of shells
of men into the air.
                        Jumpcut

to a roar, a topple of pots
and scullions, spits and pig fat into
a shriek, into the storm, stone rooms askew

and on the slide, heartbursting drop
into the black, an egg still
perfect in a hand, a plummet of cooks

to choke on salt.
                        Blackberry eyes
saw that. What did they see? The fulmar
planes on by. The gulf stares on.

Blue tit on a fennel head

Do you see me, you unafraid
feathered scrap of nothing clinging to
the fennel head, your life on fade?

Though you strop your tiny beak, the round
jet of your eye glints and you swallow
fennel seeds, you must be for the ground.

Nothing else could excuse this amazing
calm in the face of my face
looming in like a moon gazing.

How dare you flaunt me your white
eyelids, yellow back, as close as this,
you whom every movement pricks to flight?

I see your minuscule knuckles curled
round a thread of stalk; and you see,
perhaps, nothing whatsoever of my world.

All is on my side: wonder, awe
and questions. Your black eye seeks only
truth of the full seedhead, the kestrel's claw.

Mountaineer

Dead fly travels the floor, meekly
bowed in insect death's neat crouch.
Live-wire ant jerks, works the giant
load back and back. Minutes stretch;

shade to sun to shaded foot of a
low wall, four bricks high. Incredible
feat of vertical effort, up over
ravines of mortar, tumps of clay bubble,

rough scree of dust. Backwards, backwards;
jaws a breath could break, clamped round
an elephantine leg; a frantic will
clenched against weakness, puff of wind,

outrush of a spider, flick of an idle
finger. Close, my lens shows a varnished
cobalt egg of abdomen, hair-like
legs scrabbling for holds. What's in that polished

pin of a head stays hidden as it drags
the crouched fly into dark. But something lingers,
out in the light, of distance bridged by climbing
mountains in the company of strangers.

Donkey dawn

Before the sun begins to glow
on valley fields or mountain snow,
before the day is truly born,
Thronos awakes to donkey dawn.

I lie cocooned inside the deep
contentment of a sweet night's sleep,
until I hear that first forlorn
unearthly sound of donkey dawn.

How pleasant it would be to glide
to morning's shore on songbirds' tide,
instead of being rudely torn
out of my dreams at donkey dawn.

I jerk awake when first I hear
that opening, long-drawn, brassy blare –
no Cretan driver honks his horn
more stridently than donkey dawn.

A breathless silence then ensues,
as at receipt of awful news;
a second's hush, that soon will spawn
the real row of donkey dawn.

Is that a smoker being sick
with laboured heavings hoarse and thick?
Or is it timber being sawn
inside my head at donkey dawn?

It sounds as if the village pump
is being worked with wheeze and bump,
slowly, with handles old and worn,
by sadist fiends at donkey dawn.

And now the roosters raise their din,
and all the village dogs join in;
the last vestige of peace is shorn
from hill and grove at donkey dawn.

I will not stand it one day more;
my bags are packed and at the door;
by all the curses I have sworn,
I will be quit of donkey dawn.

Yet when I wake in Bristol town,
where noisy cars roar up and down,
and students vomit on my lawn –
I'll miss the sound of donkey dawn.

Pig joke

It was on Whitchurch Hill, a place
rightly called The Wilderness; a saddleback
of grey ground edged with trees and slabbed
with tractor-sliced mud, more than my boots
could ride over.
              Pigs had colonised
this no-man's-land with admirable thoroughness,
a visigoth blitz on the colour green.
Whatever had been edible here they had
utterly eaten, yet still snuffled with their
rubbery snouts to the earth, truffling
for God knows what.
              Skidding by, I liked
the comical look of them. I chuckled at the
humorous twist of pig mouths, curvilinear
ironic grins that cracked the mud masks;
the pale amused eyes.
              Next moment
I was on my face. Icarus
flopped in the ocean, Ozymandias the Great
crashed in the sands: a lord of creation
arse over tip.
              Pigs are not ironists;
they are pigs, earthy and practical;
mud millionaires. They did not see the joke.

The cricket

The cricket hung without moving
inside the porch on the green
paintwork of the back door;
an eyeless sliver of carapace,
of spiked mechanical rods and wires.
It clung all day, making no move
towards the nesting spiders or the
open window: grass-coloured, silent.

I knew what was best for the cricket:
the shelter of grasses, sunlight, the outdoors;
what I should want, were I a dry
uncommunicative insect.

Into a box I gently knocked
the cricket, tipped it on a warm
rock at the cliff edge and went
on about my business, cutting
sandwiches, drying the bathing suits.
I smiled whenever I thought of the
cricket saved in the sunshine, freed,
unknowing of its benefactor;

while black-backed gulls hissed
over the cliff and the dark
intent vee of a kestrel
hung without moving overhead.

LIGHT AND DARK

'STRANDBEEST DANCE' – Strandbeests ('beach animals') are the brainchildren of Dutch artist and inventor Theo Jansen. Strandbeests are huge, wind-powered creations that resemble skeletal dinosaurs, many of them composed of hollow plastic tubing. Some have sails, some have wings or propellers, some have scoops with scalloped edges – all to catch the wind and funnel it down to the intricate 'nerve cell' mechanisms that transform it into motive energy. It is Theo Jansen's dream to set flocks and herds of his beests free on the sandy beaches of his native coast, to run up and down at the whim of the wind. One branch of the evolutionary tree of the Strandbeests is occupied by a lumbering, tank-like brute as big as a house by the name of Animaris Rhinoceros Transport that looks as if it's out to rule the world. Of all the beests, though, my own favourite is a gorgeous, rippling monster called Currens Ventosa. I was absurdly pleased when Theo Jansen promised to insert a copy of 'Strandbeest dance' into one of her tubes, to accompany her henceforth everywhere she walks on those windy North Sea beaches.

'THE DARK ARCHES' – I first visited Leeds on a harsh Marsh evening in 1969, and my internal picture of the city was fixed from then on as grim and dark, a Gothic waste of stark black factories, cobbled slushy lanes under lamplight, and hoarse threatening shouts from nearby streets. It seemed a city clogged with soot and litter, its people on an eternal trudge with hunched shoulders into a sleety gale. Returning on a bitter snowy day in 2001, I found myself walking through the 'Dark Arches', a vaulted catacomb under a railway viaduct through which the River Aire rushed with an angry hiss and blast of cold river breath. Smart new shops and disco beats filled the Dark Arches, symptomatic of a Leeds that had changed a long way in those 30 years. But a sinister murmur of the past still clung to the aptly named 'Dark Arches'.

'THE BURGER COOKS' was written on 10 September 2001 as I waited at Heathrow Airport for my son to arrive from Australia. We did not know, of course, that the world was about to change.

'THE WALL' – The light of civilization, as the Romans saw it, gave way to the dark of barbarism at the gates of Hadrian's Wall.

'JANE READING BY TORCHLIGHT' – Dogs seem to do duty in my psyche as symbols of inchoate terrors; a curious thing, since I like dogs and they like me.

Strandbeest dance

Currens Ventosa, rackety clatter of a
ramshackle animal taps the wet
Friesland air and sand. Forty knees
crook and crack; she bows and tittups to
her own ghost face, her spider bones
scamper. Let her lightly dance, her wings
ripple and churr and lift her away
over the spray into the wind and day,

over the glum thumping of Rhinoceros,
the hollow martial shuffle and the thunder
and the weight of night. You hunched bad
beest, you glowerer; lift your black snout
where shimmering Ventosa dances and
up from dark matter leaps light.

The Dark Arches

Out of the snow, in where the river
blows cold. The city's Gormenghast
past seeps out of these vaults,
plug what gaps you wish along the canal.

Tamp it down, smooth it off with
wine shops and rocket salad. Tune the
viaduct's hydra mouths to soft beats:
keynotes growl on through the Dark Arches.

Heritage: there's a word to draw
the sting from what mills really meant,
the shadows foundries cast. Wrap it in a
cosy sweater, in a ciabatta stick.

Seed the slums, the dumps. Magic away
the Leeds of black chimneys. Skate the shoppers,
the eaters, over hell holes. Remember
the Dark Arches under the pretty snow.

The burger cooks

Groomed beyond anything that looks
real, tall cool works of art
crafted at small mirrors, a pair
of ponytailed girls graze apart.
Around them a greasy scurf of cooks
slaps out burgers, airport fare

not for these fine fillies. They
have eaten with the gods in sky fields
five miles above the Gulf. Their haunches
quiver; constrictive shoes strain their heels.
The shapeless cooks slap, prodding fat grey
meat about the hotplates, ogres' lunches.

The hostesses have touched our earth swooning
out of Dubai and some pilot's bed,
some fabulous rider. Such particular races
are for the insider: so says the red
flash of their ribbons and their gold lining,
and the grey glaze of the cooks' faces.

The wall

This wall that I follow from Windshields to
Sewingshields is a fake. These stone hackles
raised along the buckled back of the crags
are not the Wall.

Whatever the squaddies raised under some
cursing centurion lies long scattered by
animal treading. Ewes heavy with unshorn coats,
irresponsible lambs and the barn-builders who
owned them took it all apart.

A wall is a fact – yet this stretch
along whose blocks I rattle my stick
is pure guesswork. A legion's
masons squared these stones, for sure; but
who can place the cohort's placing of them?

Yet I do not distrust this cobbled-together
jigsaw stab at the block between dark and light.

The wall does not merely lead me safe to
wherever I am to sleep tonight.

Clouds cross the sun's glance northwards over
debatable ground. I blow on my hands and lean,
staring from the crags, seeing
mild grazing and settled farms full of
corn and many shadows on the move.

Jane reading by torchlight

Dreams cloud behind me, but the book glows.
A long downland slope, this climb
of the curve of an arm, all that's lit,
rising to a crescent shoulder. Time
lies moon-mazed in some hollow
a long way from here. And I lie
moonstruck and dreamstruck inside
the lisp of each page turned, each shift and sigh.

Not words: only a painter could
catch such peace. Do not snatch me back,
dream hounds I have run from, sly night.
This soft word-circle, its satellite
slope of an arm are what I hold to,
struggling earthward out of a dark wood.

HOBGOBLINS

F EAR – I have run far and wide from that belittling emotion. Fear in the face of dogs, of horses, of stormy hills, of leaping into water: it wells from a place too deep to reach by thinking. It is I who stalk myself along with the mist and nightfall on a lonely mountain track, or come galloping at myself across a field with teeth bared. I should have learned that lesson thoroughly by now, and yet hobgoblins still wait round the bend.

'THOSE DOGS' – Savage wolfhounds of the mind haunted and daunted me before my long walk through the remote mountains of Crete. Meeting them on the ground, I found that a brandishing of my stick or the offer of a piece of *paximadia* rusk bread invariably did the trick.

'PENDLE TOLL' – Pendle Hill on the Lancashire moors has a sombre reputation. It is subject to furious mood swings, sudden blizzards and rainbursts, and was the scene in 1612 of a clutch of well-documented tragedies, when ten local women and men were hanged at Lancaster for witchcraft. The persecution and bizarre confessions, the alleged murderous practices of Alizon Device, Chattox, Old Demdike and other ominously named dwellers in the shadow of Pendle Hill, have sullied its name with a sinister and long-lasting stain. Yet this hilltop was also where the young itinerant preacher George Fox, fired with spiritual energy and brimful of nonconformist zeal, experienced an epiphany in 1652, hearing the command of God to go forth and gather 'a great people'. Fox did just that, founding the Society of Friends or Quaker movement, and preaching with passion and huge bravery all over the north of England.

'AT BEAVER FALLS' – Quaking on a narrow rock ledge at Beaver Falls, down in the nethermost depths of the Grand Canyon, I watched a young girl leap fearlessly into the river 50 feet below.

'THE MARE' – The extraordinary Encamisa night-time festival in the village of Navalvillar in Extremadura, central Spain, takes place every 16 January, the feast of San Anton, and involves at least 500 over-excited horses being galloped between flaring bonfires through the narrow, cobbled and crowded streets amid volleys of firecrackers. Not exactly a relaxed environment for someone who gets anxious if the most docile dobbin approaches him in a paddock. Yet when I found myself gripped by the collar and trouser seat and thrown aboard one of the charging horses, a strange and quite unwarranted calm descended. Somehow the febrile atmosphere, the heady smells and sounds, the wine and the irrepressible affirmation of life, loud and rude, had combined to drive away my fears.

Those dogs

Those dogs that writhe black lips back
from traps of teeth, that burst their chains,
that prowl the tracks thirsty for blood
the colour of mine, that leap fences,

scale walls, gallop the hills
with lolling tongues dripping; dogs
that snarl and hackle, tear and rip;
dogs adrift, abroad, aflame

with killing lust: I know those dogs,
have nurtured them, have laid them on
my trail myself. Every hour,
on every path, I will outface them.

Pendle toll

Traveller's baulk, Pendle Hill weighs
massively over my heart.
Haunted whaleback in a grey afternoon,
this is not any of my wish
which is to be bold tomorrow
breasting the ridge, a map and compass man
bone headed, stone hearted.

Pendle, I have heard nothing but
ominous news, of spells of storms,
and of spells. It is not your puckered
flank, sucked in like a shocked breath,
that grows these eldritch seeds, but
the leaden sky, the bruised cloud
within, dread's pale template.

Now the elliptical toll of Pendle,
the bell-like thud of a heart that may
crumple to a witch's rake, or
spring boldly out of baulk;
then the pilgrim stride atop the
hill, sounding the day of the Lord
in the face of all hobgoblins.

At Beaver Falls

So she leaped into the canyon
as she said she'd do. Go, Tilke, go,
you salmon of a girl, out to where
there's no hold but on the little
finger of God.

Go for us who cling, crabbed to
the niches we've clawed to and
aching; go how we'd mean to,
chin to the wind, not outfacing but
embracing the falls,

outjumping the old sad sack, time.
So she did, on self-assembled wings; launched
her flight through air and water,
oxygenated, a firmament leaper, in a
salmon curve shining.

The mare

Walking her home, the sweaty mare
shivering under frosty stars,
I sing, having faced down
a lifelong nightmare, dread of the horse –
skull faces, thunderous slamming
of hoof drums, flick and flash of silvered
shoes – dream horses, merely.

I press my shoulder into the mare's
flank. Her plumed breath smokes
the stars and blurs stocky Antonio
limping ahead. Her skin shudders,
an eyeless lid blinking across the
veined musculature, filling
and emptying at every pulse of blood.

Now I can face it. Stroking, I see
what the rip of firecrackers
in Navalvillar's alleys, the fiesta's
wineskin roar woke when
among the fires she galloped us
from madness to madness: the hot ebb
and flow of a shared tide, life.

FESTIVAL

Festivals are by no means all jollification and bonhomie. There can be dark as well as light in them: witness the torching of evil Ravana at the culmination of the Hindu festival of Navratri, the bare-knuckle fights that take place behind the hedge around Priddy Sheep Fair on Mendip, or the traditional rough play at celebrations such as Dingle Wren on St Stephen's Day in south-west Ireland, and the famous and bruising Bottle Kicking on Easter Monday at Hallaton in Leicestershire. Dark or light, festivals seem to draw forth the essential characteristics of their celebrating communities. Cretans at their village saints' days become even fiercer and friendlier; Cadiz carnival revellers pillory their public officials with even more zeal than they do in everyday gossip; a bloodthirsty ferocity coalesces around the bearded and howling 'Vikings' who burn a longship by night in the falling snow of January during the Shetland midwinter festival of Up-Helly-A'.

'PRIESTS DANCING AT PETROHORI' – My dear friend Lambros Papoutsakis invited me to the feast in his native village of Petrohori, high on the hill slope on the eastern side of the Amari Valley in central Crete. The Amari, a fertile green haven under the mighty horned mountain of Psiloritis, is so fruitful and so hospitable a place that wartime British officers who were liaising with the Cretan resistance fighters christened it 'Lotus Land'. Many villages here were burned and their inhabitants shot in reprisals carried out by the German occupiers of Crete from 1941–4, but the resisting spirit never faltered among a people who have been invaded and occupied by successive foreign powers for the past 4,000 years, but have never been conquered by any of them.

'WOLVES OF PORTO SANTO' – I visited the semi-barren Atlantic island of Porto Santo, 400 miles from the West African coast, during the annual feast of Sao João in late June. Porto Santo's grey and yellow slopes of powdery volcanic soil rise to high mountain peaks, sparsely forested with pine trees. The bare stone-walled terraces and deep erosion gullies speak eloquently of Porto Santo's deforestation several centuries ago by pirate settlers.

'AFTER THE GAME' – From a Funchal hotel window I watched this sad little scenario unfold one night during the Euro 2004 football tournament, as the Portuguese island of Madeira celebrated the semi-final victory of their national team over fierce rivals Spain, a 1–0 win that sent Portugal through to the final.

'ROYAL INCIDENT OF THE BLIND' – A serendipitous blunder by the tube train announcer – or was it my deteriorating hearing?

'KING LAUGHTER' – A memorable communal attack of the giggles during a party.

'SPORTING LISBON' – Another football celebration; they seem to bring out the pagan rioter in the Portuguese national character.

Priests dancing at Petrohori

In the covered place by the church
two priests dance. The plump one with the
smile trails a grey hem.
His brother-in-Christ, pigtailed, pale and precise,
has neatly tucked up his black skirts.

Petrohori feasts. I raise my glass to kiss the
snowy cheeks of great Psiloritis, guardian mountain,
as Lambros unchained has kissed mine.

Smack clay dust from your shoe soles, you
young Petrohori farmers. Tense whining of
lyra, foxy glances of the players
judge your moment faultlessly,
the skyward flight of feet and spirit

beyond what your fathers aspire to, or your shuffling
grandfathers, sappy old men crooking
arthritic knees, swinging polished boots in the dance.

Linking old ones and young step the well-matched
brothers, soberly, black shoes held to the dust.
Some day, following tradition, wolves may
again menace the flock. Then priestly soles
will rouse the clay once more round Petrohori.

Wolves of Porto Santo

Dry terraces crease Porto Santo's face
with hardship lines. Dust on the bone
of the high gullies, a naked place.

Sea wolves did this, rovers turning
cutlass to hoe, the green island
greyed and flayed between lop and burning.

Night lanterns cut to the bare
bedrock, through to the bone, out from these
joyful singers caught by the flare

and shades of festival breaking forth
the olive skins of Barbary and the blue
horizon-searching stare of the north.

After the game

Beat of fado and of horns; in every
islandman's mouth the name of Gomes;
klaxons of Funchal gleefully
punching at the Atlantic night.

I looked over the wall and saw
the little group, three policemen writing
hard and apart, and those disconsolate
they listened to; a blue light turning;

shadow in the road across the course
of the revellers, a sandbank
round which the joyous river
split and remade itself and onward charged.

Royal Incident of the Blind

'A light for the Royal Incident of the Blind,'
called the announcer at Euston Square.
There came a glow; the train ceased to grind;
a bird sang and all the girls looked fair.
Everyone agreed it had needed saying
and would be heeded. Everybody smiled
at everybody else; inspectors went playing
melodeons, strangers embraced; wild
men stopped swearing and everyone
burst out cheering. The lame tossed away
their sticks, dumb men crowed the sun,
and the blind strode up into a golden day.

King Laughter

King Laughter saw that all guards were
down, and came on with a
rush. We never heard the sly

click of his boarding ladder.
His muffled shoe crossed the wall and
he was in. First to go was

the piano player, split across
the face at an unexpected
major seventh – Halleluiah the blues!

Then a dancer burst from her
buttons, doubled at the midriff.
Mother-in-law shrieked – why wouldn't she?

King Laughter crashed on through.
The wit with the wine, stabbed in the
side, clutched his wound. Rude boys

snorted as wind belted
out of gobs and guts. Roars
from the jolly chorus, poleaxed

where they drank, wine spurting
between their teeth. Pastry fragments
spattered the carpet, the guitarist

spilt beer in the piano. So passed
the king – or god, more to the point –
the laughter god, with his bright

irresistible attack.
Tearful in the wreckage, we
paid him tribute, and then some.

Sporting Lisbon

This anything-goes night, stiffsuited Antonio
must sweat in scarves. Wild men drape him lovingly,
scream like tyrants from the stadium's democracy,
commandeer his microphone for their one
roaring manifesto: SPORTEENG! SPORTEENG!

The streets go screeching. This back lane bar
seethes like a tank of maggots.

Players in their bath: the leering lens a
champagne-spattered peeping tom on naked
antics. Chubby Antonio pop-eyed
among wet underpants, another scarf
sadistically donated to wrap his cheerless grin in.

Green giant enraged with glee. Blocks the bar door,
brandishes a bludgeon of flag – SPORTEENG! – is gone.

Antonio in the traffic, muffled, sweaty,
microphone to windows, bypassed. Zoom in:
crazed girls in green garlands, a fat man
collapsed in a fountain, a ribboned dog tearing at its muzzle;
fingers rousing every horn in Lisbon.

The old black watchseller enters. Nods as if
acknowledging some friend, though known by no-one.

With gritted grin, Antonio under a green cap
crowned lord of misrule, the holy fool
scarved into iconhood. We fade on
hooded shapes rollerblading down Avenida da Liberdade,
leaping among the horns and garlands, antlered, unmistakable.

WILD

THE POTENT symbolic figure of the Green Man with his hair and beard of leaves has been a favourite subject of church craftsmen for many centuries. He hides in the shadows, up among the beams or clamped to the top of a column. He spews foliage and fruit from his mouth, more rarely from nostrils, ears or eye-holes. Or he lurks among leaves, peering forth, a secretive and sinister watcher. His expression is solemn, preoccupied, often cynical or pained – almost never joyful. No-one knows who or what the Green Man signifies. If he symbolises Christ and the fruitful word, it is a Christ with a strikingly pagan undertone. Perhaps it is the light and dark facets of the human soul. Though the metaphor must have been common knowledge among medieval sculptors and those they sculpted for, it has long been lost.

'GREEN MAN AT NAYLAND' – Although I lived in the village of Nayland on the Suffolk/Essex border for six years, I never even noticed the wonderful, sullen Green Man frowning in the rafters of St James's Church. Long after I had left Nayland my friend Tim Shackleton sent me a photograph of the sulky, scowling face, with solidly carved vine leaves and bunches of grapes issuing from its mouth to form a frame for the blunt head. Tim's photograph, which graces the cover of this book, inspired Andrew Davidson's beautiful frontipiece woodcut.

'UNDERPINNING' – The boat-like crypt of Lund Cathedral in southern Sweden holds a fine stone carving of the ogre Finn, grasping a pillar as if trying, Samson-like, to pull down the building.

'HOLLOW' – I never found the standing stone on Slayfonn. But the resonance of the stormy, threatening day of my climb up there, beyond the Vale of Glendalough in Ireland's Wicklow Hills, brought to mind an eerie, half-rotted wickerwork model of mad King Sweeney that I had found in a holly tree at Birr Castle in County Offaly a few days before.

Green Man at Nayland

Old man, who has been torturing you?
Someone has pulled a forked branch tongue
from roots down in your throat, gaggingly deep.
If you had eyes, they're empty now. He cut you
gnashing from the trunk, pegged you up among

faces gurning fit to make the Devil
wish he'd stayed away. There has been anarchy
at play in this ordered place, playfulness
with a twist of greenwood dark: that frown,
shading your vampire grin, says as much.

How are we supposed to take your meaning,
old wormpoxed genius of the upper
shadows? Do you offer these shoots as salvation,
love as green leaves, blood-rich grapes;
or only mockery, the blankness of tanglewood?

Underpinning

'Have you a Green Man?' The pastor's
hand shoots out. A misericord
thumps back; the glare scowls there
under the noses and the arses of
the clergy, for a tease or
to bind in a greenwood strength.

The pastor shares me a smile,
badge of the green brotherhood.

Beneath us, in Lund's
orlop of a crypt, Finn the ogre
grasps his pillar, the gross old
villain struck stark for trying
to shake the great stone ship
to bits, angered when the bells
woke him from a mossy dream
of love – or maybe Lund's
hero at the roots, pledged
for all time, holding all together.

Hollow

Mad birdfoot skeleton, Sweeney lodged
in a holly crown and
staring down. Who pegged him there knew
the horror of the hollow.
Wicker teeth, claws, twig flicker,
man to bird to tree

emptying. At winter druids torched
contagious kin in
wicker under stars. Built vegetable
prisons, cremational
giants crammed full on the hilltops.
Fever running riot,

sick men burning. Snow and ashes flew,
whole men howled.
This I found in the hollow on the
head of Slayfonn,
looking for a rumoured
standing stone with a black gale blowing.

REDEMPTION

B EING A BORN ANGLICAN, signed-up Catholic and practising ecumenicist in an era of lines drawn in the sand and defences fanatically manned, I have found myself travelling in interesting times. I have said prayers in ruined monasteries and on mountain tops, walked Hindu pilgrimages, sung evening praises with Baptists and morning ones with Wee Frees. I have argued with monks and libertines, been harangued simultaneously by Protestant and Catholic fundamentalists in an Armagh pub, laughed with Muslim friends, played tunes to raise the devil, laid tingling palms on standing stones, heard heavenly music while drinking from holy wells and illicit stills. Such threads of faith, old and new, secular or otherwise, seem inextricably woven into places and people.

'ON THE SCARS' – written in the Northumbrian village of Seahouses after a trip to the Farne Islands where St Cuthbert lived in the late 7th century as a hermit, wrestling with demons.

'THE GUESTMASTER' – Brother Gildas, a man bearded to the waist, with a soft voice and a most tremendous laugh, was Guestmaster when I visited the Cistercian monastery on Caldey Island off the Pembrokeshire coast of South Wales.

'WESLEY COMES TO PREACH' – Inspired by *Where I Used To Play On The Green*, Glyn Hughes's novel about the advent of Methodism in the Calderdale district of West Yorkshire, I spent a long time tracking down Hardibutts Farm where the wild Scots pedlar William Darney would preach to packed congregations of poor textile workers, at grave risk of a beating or worse if caught. These days Hardibutts is no more than a ruin, Darney forgotten, and Hughes's remarkable book out of print. But Methodism has spread all over the world.

'JAMES CUMMINGS, MC: 15.8.20–26.10.90' – On the crest of Black Law in the Pentland Hills a little south of Edinburgh I found the Covenanter's Grave, a poignant spot where a Covenanter or out-lawed religious dissenter, John Carphin, was clandestinely buried in November 1666 by the local shepherd, Adam Sanderson. Carphin had stumbled into Sanderson's house mortally wounded after a skir-mish with dragoons. The Covenanter's Grave is a well-known walkers' landmark; but further down the hill I came across another memorial unmarked on any map. 'James Cumming, MC. 15.8.20 – 21.10.90,' read the lettering. MC – did that stand for Military Cross? This man would have been the right age to have earned one during the Second World War. There was no other clue about him. The questions came welling up. Who was he? Did he love these wild purple moors? Was this a memorial to a man buried elsewhere, or was James Cumming at rest below my boots, under these sedge clumps?

'SWEETWATER' – A chance encounter on Sweetwater beach in south-west Crete, just before Easter 1999.

'CHRIST COMES TO KILLOUGHTER' – Killoughter lies forgotten a few miles south of Dublin, a deserted railway station set back from low cliffs and a pebbly strand. A moody shore.

On the scars

They are thick with salt and
salty, the weed and the blood
branching in the flood, the green
fronds and the red.

Was it a devil threw you from the cliff
down on the scars? Your torn
toes have smeared the rocks, the coarse
leather of your sealskin shoe.

Lie quiet with your
scowl in the pool and you will
join the lover who drove you here
before the heart beats thrice.

You palm down the barnacled scars
of Farne, pull back your face for
that roar of a gasp that brings the beast,
life, clawing. Your lover holds

no sponge, no hyssop. Here's the cold
anaesthetic of the wind,
a hungry heart, and the climb
of a crag that always steepens.

The Guestmaster

The Guestmaster's big round body
strains his shirt. Stub hands cup
the pale cheeks, lodging fingers like birds
in a beard thicket under black
thunder brows.
                           His gentle voice asks
about tea. He's hospitality
built solid, a Green Man grounded,
well tempered through all the island
has visited on him.
                           'That first night
I wept in my cell over the cold silences,
the abbot's wordless brush of a blessing.
Only the island held me, God's
prison in water.'
                           One senses birds
stark in a stripped thicket, every kind
of bone-bare openness. Sharper than
winter or a Danish sword, those quiet
questions of God.
                           'I have been an empty
sounding skin, drummed by demons. Now
I press my ear to a tree and hear
branches meshing to the wood's end,
interconnections; the cupped hands of God
and the island, my hands.'

Wesley comes to preach

It is the barking of the Hardibutts dogs
tells them of the hard man's coming,
the chestnut mare in the long wet lane.
He's two foreign folk with him, black
looking chaps striding through the puddles.

Wild Darney the doomsman is already
hidden in the house, shaking rain from
the briar beard, cracking his red knuckles
over the fire. His stinking bundle lies
sodden from Black Sike Hill and the

fall he got there. Stains on the tattered
sacking: brown from peat, and blotched black
of inky words watered from the tracts
that splutter out of Darney. The pedlar sings
asthmatically: he will write more

should the man who is coming leave
any breath in the swart old body
when his business be done. The riders reach
in out of the lane, looming out of steam,
making the dogs rave at chains' end

and the hunted man stiffen at the fire.
The shippon in the yard squares like
a green stone fortress; eyes squint
from holes and chinks, and there is a deep
sigh as if the wind were bosomed there.

'James Cummings MC: 15.8.20–26.10.90'

James Cummings lies under sedge
in a curve of Black Law. I found
his enigmatic stone: a name, numbers.

What hallows this Pentland ground
must be the other, mythic presence
prickling at the nape of the hill;

the Covenanter, slain and buried. That tale
retains its biblical power to thrill,
to set sermons in stones. We see

the honest herd of Blackhill, Cyrene-like
under the weight of the fugitive and his own
conscience, every upward step a spike

in a hard-won thorny crown;
bloody legs dangling down his bowed
back. The Golgotha of Black Law;

a grave stealthily dug, no shroud
nor coffin, but a decent man's desire
to do a dead man's will: 'Bury me

where I can see my Ayrshire hills.' Later
the proper memorial slab, so all might see
how heaven deals deserts. James Cummings,

you do not speak so ringingly. What you said
as death stepped up, sedge and stone play down
till God levels the hills, levels the dead.

Sweetwater

Yesterday he checked his cache, the old
Canadian. Climbed far above the shore
into the yellow synclined cliff, rolled
away the stone and found tent, stove,
lamp, the long spade bundled in a
place apart as he'd left them. Saw
no angels, though he might have in that high
niche over Sweetwater near the sky.

Tends the beach like a gardener, his mind
seeing more than pebbles. Looks for little; makes
something from nothing. What the devil brings
he'll deal with, living stripped, seeing if
the sun can clean him, knowing how to find
under the dry stones the sweet springs.

Christ comes to Killoughter

And the trees of the field shall clap their hands,
a black clatter and susurration
down the wintering coast.
The hills shall skip and sing forth your praises
in the shatter of frost-worked rock,
the rumble of streambeds.
The high places shall be brought low
one flake at a time, bending the knee
into the wetlands' suck.
Yea, the sea shall dance tremendously
at Killoughter, pounding the grey
and red strand pebbles;
a dance of joy, Lord, a generous
glut of welcome to the hornpipe
bounce of your coracle.

Not from a scrolled-back sky will you
furiously plummet: there'll be no aghast
old goats for the burning.
The low silty cliffs carry your
weightless tread; spikenard and
myrrh shall seed there.
In the puddled lane between the
gravel pits I'll know your glance;
accept your light by the
hanging gate of the old station;
or glimpse you through the window of Paddy's
bright little pub
under wild-going trees, striding the
crests of rising hills and a
great sea roaring.

IRELAND

I LOVE WALKING and exploring the back country of Ireland, slowly and on foot, with one of Tim Robinson's splendid pen-and-ink 'Folding Landscape' maps in hand and a whole day stretching away in front of me. To dive into the deep slow pool of Irish rural time and float or swim idly there, in the limestone wilderness of the Burren hills, for example, not really hunting for wild flowers and standing stones, not quite looking for a holy well or an ancient ring-fort, not exactly going anywhere unless it's towards a corner seat among the musicians in McGann's or Linnane's – this to me is the pure drop, the absolute essence of magic.

The first of these four poems reflects that aspect of Ireland: the others tilt the mirror a different way.

'CLEANING THE GRAVE FOR CEMETERY SUNDAY' – Olcan Masterson is a wonderful traditional musician and walking companion, and a great man for unlocking all sorts of secrets from the landscapes of County Mayo. Cemetery Sunday is a rural event across Ireland; overgrown burial plots are cleaned and tidied by loved ones in preparation for an outdoor Mass, said in the cemetery in the presence of hundreds sitting on or by the graves.

'RAKISH PADDY AND THE MAJOR' – Two contrasting exhibits struck me in the Famine Museum at Strokestown House, County Longford. One is a 19th-century cartoon showing Paddy and his colleen capering barefoot and bare-arsed across the bogs – a pretty typical contemporary English view of the Irish. The other is a letter written by the Strokestown tenants to their landlord Major Denis Mahon at the height of the potato famine of 1845–9, begging for help for their literally starving families. The major responded by evicting two-thirds of his tenants and paying £4,000 to have them transported to Canada – a voyage that many did not survive. On 2 November 1847

Denis Mahon was shot dead as a reprisal, his not entirely deserved reputation as an ogre cemented for all time.

'UNTOUCHABLES' – A scene glimpsed in a back lane off the Loyalist enclave of the Shankill Road in West Belfast at the time of the Troubles.

'FECKIN' TINKERS' – A sudden, rowdy and uncontrollable invasion of a hotel in Longford's town centre one dull evening by a couple of dozen ragamuffins from the edge-of-town travellers' encampment. None had yet reached teenage, and all were as high as kites on crazy adrenaline.

Cleaning the grave for Cemetery Sunday

Olcan kneels. His hands that were releasing
light birds of reels now perform
decorous tasks.

Blades of salted grass are barbered from
his shoemaker grandfather's grave in Claggan
with neat musicianly movements.

Pennies, his own claddagh pin and
offerings the year has made – a silt of
turf, lichens, wing cases –

are scooped from the watery socket of the
one-eyed bullaun below. Into the light
the resident curestone

swims, blinking through a coppery broth;
is raised to his temple. All must be clear
for Cemetery Sunday.

There is a restless sparkle to the bay;
scabious heads dance with bees on the
Headland of the Skull.

We slip the coins and the pin back
behind the black lens of the bullaun;
they chime into the water.

Our palms, pressed to the Mass Rock
to give it a swing, tingle over a mossy
skin of animal warmth.

Whatever the weight of the dead, and whatever
their road – boated from Inishbiggle, sent
skyward in princely smoke,

dug into the shore – the music maker
will gather them on Cemetery Sunday, launching
'Out On The Ocean'

between the mountains, for himself and for
the travelling shoemaker, Martin Masterson,
from Claggan stile.

Rakish Paddy and the Major

There runs rakish Paddy, capering free
over the bog: the bare animal feet,
the blubber mouth slack with brainless glee,
a sprig of shillelagh thick enough to beat
some decent English head to paste. Beware
the bounds of rakish Paddy. Praties and buttermilk
make him inimical to lace and silk,
feed him so fierce and red and free of care.

Here sits the Major, colourless, having read
cries from Cloonahee: 'We have no food,
no potatoes, no grain. What must we do?'
Is it stone-heartedness that thins his lips?
Perhaps he sees the hard road of the ships,
the spur of tumbled thatch, as working good.
A bitter choice? The mouth gives no clue,
and did not when rakish Paddy struck him dead
out of the dark. 'O God,' was all he said.

Untouchables

I never caught the name of the street
where you hopped bare-kneed in a
rundown part of the city; a short
cul-de-sac behind shuttered premises.

Out of the dark of a doorway four
shaven-headed bullies walked tensely
past barred church and waste grounds,
each footfall sticky with shadows.

I glimpsed the flicker of your green dress
against a black 'For God And Ulster' wall,
and at the end of the road the
pale men, untouchables passing.

Feckin' tinkers

Imps are in –
'Feckin' tinkers!' –
cheeky thin
turf smoke stinkers
lords of the dance
three feet high
on the offchance
on the sly
loud and gobby
spit and hawk
rock the lobby
drown the talk
swipe the takings
sharp as tacks
smoking rakings
in the jacks
rile the porters
gobble buns
grope the daughters
smack the sons
badger and bait
young romantics
spoil their date
with saucy antics
fuss the fair
receptionist
pull her hair
pinch her list
smash a cup
whistle airs
scamper up
forbidden stairs
stealing matches
throwing passes
dropping catches
scratching arses

daft wee lot
and getting dafter
streaming snot
screaming laughter
rude and wrecking
whole place humming
'Hey! The feckin'
barman's comin'!'
bump and roar
stock car rally
out the door
and down the alley

off they race
dirt and din ...
across my face
unrolls a grin

in the bar
gloomy drinkers
tell their jar –
'Feckin' tinkers!'

CRETE

M Y 'SECOND HOME' of the spirit, the 200-mile-long Mediter-
ranean island of Crete has enchanted, infuriated, confounded
and captivated me for the best part of 15 years. I have made wonder-
ful, life-long friends there, have explored remote corners of the island
with them that I would never have found on my own, and have come
to see Crete and the fierce, funny and fantastically hospitable Cretans
as a place and a populace that may technically be part of Greece, but
are in fact a separate country and a distinct people. Much invaded,
much oppressed, but never conquered and rarely downhearted, the
Cretans and the Irish have a lot in common. You wouldn't want to
be with anyone else when the drink flows, the tall tales build and the
music fires up.

In spring 1999 I walked from end to end of back-country, interior
Crete, a 300-mile journey across the island's four mountain ranges
whose tale is told in *The Golden Step* (Haus Publishing). During
those two months the poems came rushing out as if from a blocked
spring.

'BROTHER FOX' – written on my balcony at the Taverna Aravanes,
watching an unearthly sunset light bathe the slopes of Psiloritis and
experimentally wiggling toes that had been vilely blistered by 200
miles of Cretan limestone rubble.

'ALIEN' – A feeling of isolation from the life of the places I happened
on at nightfall was something I learned to live with along the road.

'BANDOUVAS' – Manolis Bandouvas was the feared and very effec-
tive Kapetan or leader of one of the bands of *andartes* or guerrilla
fighters who made life so uncomfortable for the German forces of
occupation during the Second World War. A headstrong leader who
did not like to be curbed or advised, he also made life difficult for the

British resistance officers in Crete, and for his own people who suffered reprisals for the spur-of-the-minute slaughter that Bandouvas's men would sometimes visit on the enemy.

'PICKUPS' – A homage to the real backbone of the Cretan economy.

'EATING BROAD BEANS THE GERAKARI WAY' – Anyone walking in springtime past a Cretan kafenion with its tin tables out on the street is bound to be tempted by this agreeable adjunct to morning conversation: a cold thimble of tsikoudia (the grapeskin spirit otherwise known as raki), a flat aluminium dish of broad beans, and a little pile of salt.

'THE HEALER'S WIFE' – Nikephoros and his wife Aretousa are the healers, herbalists and wise people of Thronos. Nikephoros with his tremendous snow-white beard and leonine face is also a musician and maker of lyras, those leaf-shaped bowed instruments whose three strings, resonating against the player's fingernails, produce the scurrying tunes that accompany traditional singing and dancing.

'MORE SWEETER' – Another Cretan friend and smoother of paths is Charis Kakoulakis, a man of deep and passionate feeling. He, like most Cretans, is adept at singing a mantinade, a four-line rhyming barb, jibe, dart or canny metaphor. Mantinades are either made up on the spur of the moment, or unearthed from the vast communal store of such little songs, in order to comment on local affairs, to proclaim love of Crete, of wine or of women, or to compliment or deflate the ego of a friend – or foe.

'WAITING FOR MIDNIGHT' – Written on the eve of Easter 1999 in the Zakros Hotel at the easternmost end of Crete. In 36 hours time I was due to begin my long walk, and was suffering from a bad case of cold feet. It was probably this state of blue funk and mild depression that lent such a gloomy, inimical air to the neon-lit bar.

Brother Fox

The orange seller came to Thronos on
one of those slow afternoons
and did his stuff at the taverna table,
one shoe cocked up on a chair, lyra
whining on his knee, pelting tunes,
part of his travelling show: ladies, look –
there's plenty up my sleeve.
                    I strummed along
and got a slap and stubbly kiss. His eyes,
a sharp brown fox's, chased a broad rump.
What do you think, eh? Quick, a song
to make her look our way. White hair
as thick as springs curled from his chest, swept
out to points under his toper's nose:
a ladies' man.
                    We leaned against his red
pickup full of oranges and kept
slow banter going. Where's your wife? In England?
So much the better. Come with me and be
an orange seller for the day. We'll drink
and play like this; you'll be a novelty
the ladies won't resist. I guarantee
we'll get our hands round more than oranges.

Was it a joke, or did he read the lone
Englishman wrong, take me for a brother
fox, a predator like himself, born
to hunt warm flesh and feast till blown?

I laughed him off. Later, dreaming in
the early evening, watching a hot light
wink on the mountain, I saw his sharp
brown fox's eyes, and thought again about
his strange mistake.

Alien

Eating rabbit stifado I sucked the fiddly
bones, knuckle-deep in gravy,
too hungry for knife or fork.
Fancied myself observed: looked up to meet
wide eyes amused, abashing to the
wild man alien in his road dust.

Screams tore apart the veil;
two black cats, one rabbit bone. Demon
ferocity clawed the reasonable air;
a really mad note. Everyone laughed:
avaunt thee, Grimalkin. I sucked on,
enfranchised by something genuinely wild.

Bandouvas

Bandouvas stares over ox-horn
moustaches, under black brows, a blank
peasant face stony with intransigence.

Two brandishing *andartes* flank him
on the sidelines; but it is the deep sunk
power of Captain Bandouvas we sense.

The photograph does justice to his feared
authority: high boots crossed,
slab fingers resting on the knees

that prop his rifle. Shirtsleeved brigand,
prisoners up before him must have guessed
his one-word sentences for blond-haired boys

dropped from the sky into such capable hands.
Scuffed toetips tell of some moonlit march.
Seated while others stand, he underlines

who calls the shots: Bandouvas the chief,
sly old wolf still hiding from the search
to find the living man among the stones.

Pickups

Pickups, you plodding workers, modern mules
of Crete: you start at dawn in farmers' yards,
whinny and honk to wake the dead; you get

your share of kicks and curses; groan at loads
you somehow carry, preposterous piles of nets,
jostles of sheep or headscarfed pickers; wait

your master's will under a plane tree's shade;
kick stones at walkers with your thin-shod wheels;
rattle your old bones, toil until you die

an unmarked death, trundled down some mountain
slope to rust in a ravine. Plump
olives, good wine, fat lambs are your memorials.

Eating broad beans the Gerakari way

If you would eat broad beans in Gerakari:
pick up a pod and wag it at your friend

to make your point, using it as a long
finger extension; now you break the end,

strip a lath of fibre down one side,
and lay down the pod. Eat some bread.

Peel the other side; then use the sharper
tip of the bristly pod to scratch your head.

Throw the strips into the ashtray. Take
your cigarette, inhale, and cough until

your friend can laugh no more. Expectorate
into the street. Tip the flask and fill

your raki glass and his. Gulp. Now cough
a whole lot more. Pick up the pod and split

it longways with your thumbnail. Spill the pale
beans out on the table. Let them sit.

Select an olive from the dish. Eat it,
and spit the stone onto the growing heap.

A sip of raki now, a measured dose.
Finger the beans, stir them about; keep

looking at your friend, the girls, your glass –
anywhere but at those plump green beans.

Start on a story: but, before you do,
wipe the pod's juices on your stiff-stained jeans,

enjoy a mighty snort and hawk; then lift
a single bean towards your mouth. Now halt

its progress; reconsider; let it return
tablewards, and dab it in the salt.

Now that the rites are properly observed,
and each tradition satisfied, you may

consume it. Learn these simple rules, if you
would eat broad beans the Gerakari way.

The healer's wife

Cures come easily to the healer's
leaf-shaped hands, beautiful through use;
red spirit of beeswax to staunch

a bloody wound, fruitful stem and flower
to bring on women's bleeding. His slim fingers
stroke leaves and limbs, scatter olives in the

hospitable dish, play midwife to mountain
trees; he sees where music grows, caresses
lyras to birth, bows them into life.

The healer's wife brings him herbs,
observes the saints' days, smooths the beaten path;
knows all his secrets, keeps some of her own.

More sweeter

> *A lárga, a lárga*
> *to filí,*
> *ya na échi*
> *nostimátha*

Charis intones, shaping his
whitening moustache with the black-haired
backs of his fingers, this way and that,

glancing at me from eyes
that glare or glow with the
ebb and flow of our talk

at this laden table in
Kato Arhanes on another
firecracking Easter night, the raki

flask emptying, another
farewell shaping. Christophere, dear
brother, this mantinade says:

> 'We put the distance
> between the kisses,
> in order to make them
> more sweeter.'

Waiting for midnight

Rasping cheeks sliced like gorges,
harshly surfaced, harshly shadowed
under cold neon. Old men sat
stonefaced in the bar, a stark anteroom.

Grandmothers rolled like sailors
up stepped lanes, ballasted,
hands pendulous with red eggs,
sweet cakes, bread, gripped in blue plastic:
conception of feasts.

Hungry lads
fooled with firecrackers, priests sang
dolorously, bells mourned, cats
slunk to bones through dark doors.

Easter broke in at midnight, burst
a rocket of light from candle to candle,
face to face. Till then the cheerless
neon hid the men of Zakros,
masked them as their cards thumped down.

MUSIC AND DANCE

O F ALL THE ICE-BREAKERS between people across the world, it is music and dance that are most effective. You may not be able to speak the other person's language; cultural chasms may be huge; the colour of your skins, the shape of your bodies and the preoccupations of your lives may be entirely opposed. But let one of you break out in a little song, a few dance steps, a fragment of tune, and there will be an immediate response from the other.

It is amazing how many tunes and songs on this earth are in the keys of G or D; also how many are in 3/4 or 4/4 time, the basic rhythms of the English, Irish and Scottish traditional music imprinted in my DNA. I have learned to carry two harmonicas with me when I travel, one in G, the other in D. They are light, portable, acceptable in most forms of music – and they don't draw attention to the player, a very important factor in my case, not only because it's helpful to me to blend in rather than stand out, but also because no-one can see how clumsily I am playing. I'm a poor player, but a keen one. Reading music has proved beyond me, but I've learned to play by ear and intuition. I dance like a buffalo on hot bricks, but people don't mind. What matters most is the joining in, the willingness to throw your couple of eggs – however small, however pallid – into the communal omelette of dance and song that is continually being cooked up by local musicians in Irish bars, in Cretan tavernas, in English pub back rooms, in Swedish kitchens, Indian homes and Australian yards. Music and the dancing it drives are the great universal handshake across divides, no matter how seemingly wide and unbridgeable.

'THE FIRST OF MAY' – Rural Crete celebrates May Day with village picnics and al fresco dancing. The villagers of Thronos go up into the woods above the valley, spit-roast lamb and pork, eat and drink till their ribs squeak, and then get out the lyras and laoutos. It's a Dionysian scene.

'DEVIL'S SHILLING' – When you are coming towards the end of an Irish pub session, sometimes magic happens and the tune soars away, taking on a life of its own. An internal roar or ringing develops, something apart from the tune being played, a supplementary rush of joy and energy as propulsive as rocket fuel. Within that surge lies all that is both heavenly and devilish about music, its capacity to enrapture and enslave.

'PARALLEL LANE' – Musicians keep their own counsel and their own time. Starting time for this back-street session of flamenco in Jerez was advertised as 10.30 p.m., but it wasn't until two o'clock in the morning that the door of the *peña* or aficionados' club was pushed open and the first player slouched casually in, guitar case in hand, fag in mouth ...

'FLAMENCO MADRID' – Two sides of the flamenco coin.

'THE WHISTLE PLAYER' – Watching the masterly flute-player Brian Finnegan perform in Iona's community hall with his band Flook, the curious contract between musician and audience fascinates me. He moves us to tears, to rage, to glee, to solemnity with his skill, his soulful dexterity. We watch his closed eyes, his concentration, his air of rapture. But ... what is actually going on in his head and heart as he weaves his spell? Is he as moved as we are? Or is it just business?

'MCCONNELL'S RETURN' – You can take the boy out of Fermanagh, but ... Cathal McConnell is one of the world's great flute-players and traditional singers. One day, maybe, he will be called home to his native county.

The First of May

The older man starts. An axe blade smile
slashes his face, a fixed grin of absence.
Across his knee the lyra shivers, pours
a distillation: braided flowers, oil,
sizzle of sheep fat, Homeric sounds
and sights – clouded wine, the singing air
under the oaks, a blue strip of hills
holding the ring, a low shimmer of fire.

Now Kosti takes it. Tips his goat head
to the sky, thrashes the bow. Blood
and drink tilt the trees. A pistol cracks.
Hands tug my hair, friend or foe
plunging me to the dance. The voice of Lambros
burrows in my ear: 'Now we are mad ... '

Devil's shilling

The fiddle fires us down the runway. A flaming
jet of notes and we are launched, climbing
the rare ramp into what shapes as bliss
towards heaven's towers, beyond rhyming
or any words, beyond labels and naming:

and here the devil with cat eyes darting,
the rogerer, the roisterer, comes prancing
down the staves, patent leather cad
sneaked in by devious means. Mirrored dancing
pumps, pencil moustache and centre parting

tip us the wink, live up to his billing.
Into the tune we lean, blindly burning
round air's sweet curves, come one, come all,
too mazed with flight to care if we are earning
heaven's treasure or the devil's shilling.

Parallel lane

A slippery trap, this flamenco hour,
no sooner set than stretched. The tense clapping
of the barman's palms, of drinkers' heels
ticks it out; the hiss of a comb through
ridged gitano hair,

tap of a gold ring, glint of a watch face.
The spirit of El Terremoto stalks us,
the Earthquake Man, bullfaced belter of songs
rolling his shoulders under the earth; and of harpies
clutching us to the rack,

to a soak of sex, a cage of sweet grief.
In some other bar down a parallel
lane, blue smoke curls. The singers
throatily cough, casually chat;
guitarists yawn

into the next yarn, the glass after next.
Ours was a sundown tryst, but
believed by no-one save the anxious boy
biting his nails beneath the great Terremoto,
the pudgy god caught

in old shots with other familiars
of a song's deeps, clawing the years down.
As well set clocks to the stamping legs
of that mountainous bullroarer
bursting from his frame,

or time by the crack of a stick in a
campfire's flame, as chain such ones
down to some hour. The night ripens and
lions are there, padding towards our pool,
shadows among their hides.

Flamenco Madrid

Carboneras restaurant floorshow, 11 p.m.

Pity the man that roused you as you
stamped in the red dress, stamped,
a harpy hot and furious, grinding
the man the singer raised into the sprung
ground of the dance floor with the
red pestle of a shoe heel.
To be your grist was the blood-red
thought of each man in that room

as you hitched the red dress and turned
blood, hearts and meaning. Magic
flashed within the wood, strung to
the singer's high cries, and men you ground
into the dust now sprang ramping,
every man a bull, a skyrocket.

~

Candela bar, 3 a.m.

Beyond the smoothness of the red
dress, the polish of red heels,
this bar in the long lane where
everyone seems drained yet
waiting. Thick pine-needle stink
of kif, the barman's indolent nod
stretch out like a cat in the
Calle Olmo. Here smokers float

beyond blood and rockets, a slow
appreciation as the door swings.
Here walk gods, whitefaced and
yawning from their shows, to drink themselves
real and with scarred hands steal
fire for the faithful out of the holy wood.

The whistle player

Over the red lips tautened and under
the tough crop, fronting the mind's automated
smithy, this eye. Green of cockle beach

sand under shallows, with sea's transparency
and depth, yet blank as bottle glass
worked on by sea. The spade-tipped

fingers skitter on spouts, invisible
columns dervishing up from the whistle's
blow-holes. The tune is launched; lives. Now

the lid drops from its sheath, a screen
to throw a private magic on. He sees
nothing and no-one through the sea glass

turned in the skull, refracting the soul's
forge fire. Cradled to a chink, the blind
green eye, seeing all behind its wall.

McConnell's return

They came for Cathal: the rushy bogs, small fields,
steamy pubs, the net of puddled roads
round Bellanaleck.
                At Trory jetty
on Lough Erne's shore they set him free,
glasses askew, shucked like a caddis
from his old suit, its baggy pockets
streaming timetables, reminders, tickets, clocks
and shackles: a long procession.
                He did not shiver
in the skinning wind, the flute in his
newborn fingers.
                The boat rowed him
to a lodging under the conical roof
of the round tower on Devenish Island,
high among wild stone heads:
Fermanagh's muezzin.
                Tunes streamed from the
tower at the wind's tug, awakening the
twenty townlands and the hundred islands,
unfastening the thousand ears of God.

WAITING

A MISCELLANY OF POEMS with a loose theme. The tension of waiting, of being in that space between departure and arrival, is something that pervades the life of a travel writer and resonates in all sorts of situations.

'THE HALLELUIAH CHORUS' – An incident that took place during an Advent performance of 'The Messiah' in Wells Cathedral.

'OPEN SEASON' – I happened across this scene during the penultimate day of my long walk through Crete in 1999.

'THE SHELL' – A picture of my dear father-in-law, Matthew Rasell, on the last afternoon of his life.

'GOING TO THE RIVER' – The setting is the abandoned lead mine on Allenshields Moor in West Durham; the traveller is Will Atkinson, inspirational Northumbrian musician and shepherd, of whose death I had just heard.

'ST KEVIN AMONG THE MINERS' – I became aware of St Kevin (AD 498–618?) when walking at Glendalough in the Wicklow Hills south of Dublin, where he lived as a hermit and built a monastery. Glendalough is a deep, shadowy valley of two narrow lakes, at the head of which lie old abandoned lead workings. Kevin was famous as a communicator with animals and a healer, and also as a man of hot temper, liable to lash out. Legend says that he drowned a girl in the Glendalough lake after she had 'tempted' him in his cave.

Halleluiah Chorus

She crumpled forward, soundlessly.
Bysitters lugged her by her ankles
and wrists, limp like a shot
deer, tumbled from dignity.
Jackets were shucked and coats spread
on the cold flags and they
laid her grey-faced on this
rough, Christmas-coloured bed.

As we rose to the choir
bursting the Halleluiah Chorus
ecstatically over us,
they waited, kneeling in a low
painter's light, humbly, as though
watching a babe in a byre.

Open season

Cross swish of the girl's broom swirls
water across the terrace where her father,
having painted half the empty pool,
yawns over coffee.
                        In the angry
tide she raises, last year's leaves
flop from step to step. Plastic chairs
stand stacked; thin lawns seethe
to the clock-like tick of water sprays.

She declared open season
this morning when I blew in. Thud
of my pack by the reception desk
heralded summer over her hammer's thump,
fixing flex.

A quiet bit of coast,
shabby enough with its shanty towns,
flimsy greenhouses ripped and rickety:
hardly a beach, never a brochure star.

'Baba!' the girl snaps at her father,
having spotted the gardener slacking under
a carob tree. It's hard to keep cooing
here where tomatoes outweigh tourists;
doing women's work and men's work too,
holding things together.
                        So she scolds,
sweeping like a fierce wind breaking out
between the devil and the deep blue sea.

The shell

Dark as a mussel shell, your cold hand,
its ricepaper skin rucked in
rows of tiny wavelets, tightens
round mine, smooths to a calm.
There's a pressure, some dry communication.

The women's fingers stroke your hair, the folds
of your swimmer's face in its breathless drift
under the combers. You feared the sea
over these winter months; now you lie
cradled in a tide of fingers and murmurs,

a Sussex man, a clay-handed grower
of beans, floating away from the downland farms,
flint and seed glinting in the furrows.
We'll plant a beech for you somewhere high and
sunny, a scallop shell among its roots.

Going to the river

When the traveller touched down between
the leadmine chimneys on Allenshields Moor
he was a little out of the track
for his kind. Maybe he had taken
the moor's roll for the old river

he had always understood must be
crossed. Perhaps it was the gaunt fumestacks
rising so improbably from
the blue heather and the green lichens
delicately edged with scarlet, an ancient
time upon clouded hills now resonating.

By the dry pan of Sikehead Dam
he folded the wings, settling them to
his sides with a curlew's shiver,
smoothly enough. Was he supposed to know
the wherefore of wings, the way to the border?

No questioning that or anything else
under this new press of light and the
fading of solid things. He would make
time for one sweet rant blown to the
rocks and the raw wind; then a last
touch of the hills, and on to the river.

St Kevin among the miners

The red deer are aware of him, the little
wild figure ghosting from the rocks.
Down at the leadmill they do not hear,
over the thump of hammers and swish of the wheel,
any stone clicking. Nor do the deer.

Kevin slinks to the furnace fire – not for
its heat, there's no warming his old bones now.
The miners steam. Their thick hair drips. They face
what monks do, with bloody-minded grit:
heart-breaking work, pain in a hard place.

The bunch of nettles drags at his belt. He sees
the girl's eyes in shock, her blistered cheeks,
his righteous hand a bitter five-headed dart.
Love them all, Kevin, they told him,
barring heaven's gate: break your heart.

Blue lips, stripped lungs. The saint
shivers, dreams of a furnace mouth
yawning, of a molten lake. He smells
the men's sweat and nudges closer to the
animal ring. No prayers at Glendalough's wells

have wiped his slate. That must be done here
among the miners. Thirteen hundred years,
and only these blue-skinned men of the Upper Lake
are more outcast than he. The murderer
outstares the flames, sees himself wake

in the moonlit cave, his last moment
of grace. The girl's face looms, shrouded
by temptress hair. The plump lips part;
the lips of hell. Into the lake with her!
Thought to deed: one pulse of a heart

he never felt, would not own now.
His eyes spill tears to brim wells.
The wheel turns, and the hammer sings.
Among the miners Kevin trembles, feeling
an almost despaired-of unfolding of wings.

POETS

AMONG WRITERS who have inspired me tremendously are Patrick Kavanagh and Edward Thomas, both poets of landscape and the realities of country life.

Patrick Kavanagh (1904–67) was a small-time farmer in the tumbled, intimate drumlin country around his birthplace of Inishkeen in County Monaghan, until in his early thirties he left to live as a writer in Dublin and London. His poems bring the small hedged fields, dark soil and cloudy skies of this pinched farming countryside vividly to life for me.

Edward Thomas (1878–1917) lived mostly in the chalk and clay downland country of Hampshire, at first churning out topographical accounts and biographies for a living, then bursting into a brief flowering of poetry after being inspired to try his hand at it by his friend the American poet Robert Frost. Thomas suffered from crushing depression, which he tried to relieve by long solitary walks. He was happiest, strangely, after joining the army as a volunteer early in the First World War. Thomas was killed by a shell blast on the first morning of the Battle of Arras at Easter 1917, and is buried under a cherry tree in Agny cemetery.

'LANES OF JOY' – I wrote this poem after visiting Patrick Kavanagh's home village of Inniskeen and finding my way into the fields around Shancoduff, his farm.

'ON FIRST LOOKING INTO THE ORDNANCE SURVEY'S *GAZETTEER OF GREAT BRITAIN*' – 800 minutely printed pages of sheer delight – poetry in the raw, that only needs a bit of tweaking ...

'SITTING WITH EDWARD' – Half asleep by the fire in the Elsted Inn after a long day's tramp over the downs of the Hampshire/Sussex border, I half imagined, half dreamed that Edward Thomas was sitting tensely by me, not yet a poet, eating himself up with self-absorbed misery and frustration.

Lanes of joy

Gather bits of road, said the farmer, Kavanagh, who
was raised in a dour house on a ridge:
gather eternal lanes of joy. What a wild
thought for a lone Monaghan man. So I chose
the dark stodge of mud in the half-begotten
lane to Shancoduff.

At the track end,
in place of emaciated walls and rafters
imagination had sited there, lay three smooth fields under
a hanging wood and cows chin-deep in a bog.
No stony grey soil to curse, no
palatable whisper of melancholy
nor black hills looking north towards Armagh.

Where were the prying eyes, the starved calves huddled
under their whitethorn that had been lodged
with me like refugees? I had dug so hungrily
the rich loam of the poet's suffering: surely
he owed me a taste of the real thing?
The red and brown cows chewed on, the grass
sparkled unbegrudgingly.

Walking back to Inniskeen,
feeling the rushy beards of the fields rasp between
my fingers, I thought of the farmer in the city,
hollowed by cancer and drink, destined for
the awkward fit of fame. Burned up by
the light that lit him, 'Nature is not enough,'
he said, 'I've used up lanes' – gasping with joy
on a canal bank many miles from Monaghan.

On first looking into the Ordnance Survey's *Gazetteer of Great Britain*

Howl Beck, Roaring Middle, Groan, Moan and Yell,
Whisperdales, Mutterton, Silent Pool, Dumbrell;
Quaking Pot, Shivering Knott, Trembleath, The Scares,
Bold Burn, Brawlings, Dasher and Dares.

Leapingwells, Lightfoots, Dartmeet, The Runn,
Stamperland, Heavitree, Weighton, The Ton;
Bawdy Craig, Randy Pike, Nudge Hill, The Wink,
Stiff Street, The Risings, Soften and Sink.

Booze Moor, Tipple Cross, Drunken Bottom, Nutters,
Illers Leary, Heave Coppice, Sickers Fell, Gutters;
Gobley Hole, Gannets, Gulpher, Greedy Gut,
Shattering, Shitlington, Shothole, The Shut.

Sitting with Edward

The mud on the stockings has dried off.
You cross your thin legs, leaning back in the
angle of the bench. The clay cracks.
Tension ticks electrically along
your jaw. There are blue veins in the backs
of the hands that cradle a bony knee.
Edward, you are so eaten up,
stripped out. This is the desperate look
before Frost worked on you; papery of skin,
hollowed, jerking on that mind hook.
It must have been a thirty miler, a driven
march to a crazed compass. North by the
Shoulder of Mutton, and then where? Burned,
a seared track by Stodham, Rogate and black
paths under Trotton beeches. You have earned
the wounds stamped by the blunted nails
of your brogue soles, and the horsehairs,
impacted beech leaves and fiercely jammed
grit of the hag-ridden miles
since dawn. And still you feel dammed.
You strike me as that, a dam, building
to some bursting day. I had
expected the poet, but you are still a blocked
prose machine. I smell the metallic tang
of your fury with work mocked
by no-one but yourself. Meagre man,
I was happy scribbling by the fire till now.
You should have slept on under your cherry tree.
Did you haunt the Elsted Inn tonight
simply to shoot your spiky question at me?

PAINTERS

I WAS VERY SLOW coming to Impressionist paintings. But once I had visited the sleepy little villages on the Seine downriver of Paris where the fledgling art revolutionaries lived and painted in the 1860s and 1870s, and had followed their trail through Montmartre and Pigalle, I was completely hooked.

'ROOK BURST' – I came to Bag Enderby on the Lincolnshire wolds in search of a poet, Alfred Lord Tennyson, whose father had been Rector here in the early 19th century. But when upwards of 200 rooks suddenly exploded out of the trees around St Margaret's Church, the picture that jumped into my shocked brain was Vincent van Gogh's sinister Provençal cornfield with its ominous, oversized crows.

'SISLEY'S TRAP' – While Auguste Renoir and Claude Monet found fame and fortune (the former almost immediately, the latter in later life), their contemporary and friend Alfred Sisley stuck to land-scapes and never made a name for himself during his lifetime. He died impoverished in 1899, aged 59. Having fallen in love with Sisley's painting *The Place du Chenil at Marly-le-Roi, Snow*, I was overjoyed to find the exact spot that he had sat in 1876 to paint this dark and wonderful picture.

'LAUGHING AT CHATOU' – I wrote this on the balcony of the Res-taurant Fournaise at Chatou, a few miles downstream of Paris, where Renoir painted *Luncheon of the Boating Party* in 1881. The previous day I had viewed Camille Pissarro's *Entrance of the Village of Voisins*, painted ten years before, and felt heavy with nostalgia for those easy-paced, pre-motor car days. Renoir's straw-hatted youths and rosy-faced girls so gracefully and carelessly disposed around the restaurant balcony, Pissarro's slow horse and cart plodding up a tree-lined lane under a cloudless French sky – together the two pictures seemed to catch exactly the 19th-century Golden Age in the villages of the Seine Valley below Paris, when life moved at the pace of a rowing boat or a patient carthorse, so different from the hectic Parisian decadence captured ten years later in Henri Toulouse Lautrec's *Jane Avril dansant*.

Rook burst

I saw what I shan't forget:
two hundred rooks shot
into white air over
mud, stud and thatch. Fever
black, sharp as a bagburst.
I could not get past
this clatter of sharp panicky rooks
gunning up the sky in shrieks.
To a hot Provençal
cornfield where poplars curl
like flames, blue codes
to red and a brain reads
kaleidoscopically, that
black cousinhood belonged: but
I saw it at Bag Enderby
in a cold January,
a still day, with the wolds
curved to the sky like shields.

Sisley's trap

I set my trap in bleak weather
in the Place du Chenil and there

I caught light, the dim heavy light
of snow lying under cloudy air.

I caught Marly-le-Roi in a trap of white
and of snowy grey and of black

and blue subdued into the snow's light.
I pushed the Sun King out to the back

of the sky and I caught plain men,
trapping them on an old road in black.

In the space between now and then
I filled my trap full of gold and not

my pockets. I caught women and men
and the bright mills at Moret and the hot

smokiness of steamboats. I caught
what Claude let drop, what Auguste forgot

in fame's flush. What we once caught together
traps me on the old road in bleak weather.

Laughing at Chatou

I heard
laughing at Chatou;
bearded chuckles that went away
like smoke under a striped awning.
They curled, thickened with wine, to
rock like boats on the stippled river.
Rosy faces glowed, round, young, not
innocent exactly. Full lips, dark eyes:
immortals gathered on a balcony.

I heard
sex cries in Montmartre, sharp, desperate,
arching from a window – probably the little
horned nobleman, raking the coals where
mills ground colour from the cheeks,
money from the nightmare of
prancing whores, hollowed dancers.
Unbearably sad, such heart-squeezing
vivacity.

Poplar shadows
bar lost ways into the Seine's
humped horse-paced villages,
the heavenly days.
Gaunter than Jane Avril's
sacked city of a face, these skeleton trunks
point blackly, like guns, towards the mud.

LANDSCAPES

LANDSCAPES are a travel writer's stock-in-trade. At first it is the most spectacular – the Grand Canyon, the Himalayas, the South Sea islands – that draw the attention and whet the pen. After a while it is shades of line and mood that appeal. Evocation becomes a greater challenge than description, and the voices of a landscape – its subtleties of history and geological makeup, its idiosyncrasies, the comparisons one has learned to draw between this landscape and others – begin to make themselves heard.

'THE APPLE WIFE' – Overheard at Trieste airport, after I had been walking the First World War front line positions along the Soča Front – the Isonzo Front, as the Italians called it – which run up and along the precipitous crests and ridges of the Julian Alps where Italy and Slovenia meet. Over the course of 29 months between 1915 and 1917, on a front less than 50 miles long, over a million Italians and nearly 700,000 of their opponents – Austrians, Bosnians, Poles, Hungarians, Germans – died or were mutilated for life. The stalemate produced a campaign as bloody and terrible as that on the Western Front, but one which – apart from Ernest Hemingway's classic and romantic account of it in *A Farewell to Arms* – remains all but unknown.

'THE LEAP' – In the woods above Bolton Abbey, near the foot of Wharfedale in North Yorkshire, lies a spectacular set of rapids called The Strid. This black rock slit in the valley floor was formed by the collapse of the roof of a string of caverns hollowed out of the limestone by the River Wharfe, which rushes through the defile in a roaring, bubble-filled torrent. The lichen-coated rocks are treacherous, and many have drowned trying to leap the gap.

'BOY IN WET BOOTS' – I grew up in the flood-plain of the River Severn near Gloucester, a flat country that flooded every winter, then froze into an immense skating and sliding rink. It couldn't have been a more exciting landscape for a little boy to run about freely in, and I'm sure it made me a writer.

'THE OUTBACK ROADS' – A glimpse from an aeroplane flying over the central Australian outback between Darwin and Alice Springs. The ruler-straight dirt roads of the 'whitefellers' are the most obvious things visible from 20,000 feet; the Aboriginals' trails, integral with the landscape, lie hidden from uninitiated eyes.

The apple wife

'Rack up the Bramleys for winter,'
the warm Worcestershire voice drifts, sweet
as applewood smoke; 'I worry about them trees.'

Comfortable body, shifting her bulk
in the hard lounge seat. 'They'll be
all rot and ruin, time we get home.'

Over the runways clouds gleam with a
sheen of snow. Above the milky Soča,
upcountry from here, Krn and Vrsič

cut their mountain heads into a sky
thick as the fruitless dead, shrugging shoulders
trenched in time with the Flanders plain.

Thunder volleys; mist swirls like gunsmoke;
metaphors grate at each rifle slit, jab
with rusty Hapsburg barbs, belch from craters.

Smeared across the screes, pulped on the
slopes, unripe crop snatched down too soon
for bedding on a mattress of straw,

for spreading of seed through barren Friuli
or the dry furrows of Carinthia.
'Reckon we'll save the best of 'em,' burrs

the apple wife, ticket in her fist,
planning for winter battened down, her
precious fruit racked out of ruin.

The leap

Windings of mist ladled like
whey on the fell and smoke
in the dale, in earth's dark old bed
and what underlies the wood.

Bubbles muscle at the black holes
of the narrows and there are skirls
out of the glassy water, not the smash
of spate nor the rumble and crush

of boulders rolling, but siren voices
deep in the river's molten races
under the trees. Who does not see
the mossy skidpan, the heartless lie

of the rocks? The beast in the walls
gulps, swallows, claws the tide, howls
blindly for a titbit. What short praise,
what vainglory, what glances from bright eyes

beguile us across black narrows, out
where the smoke and the veiled voices wait?
We leap without cause, without promise or hope
of any landing. Yet we leap.

Boy in wet boots

February flood
in over the sill.
Under the skin, like blood,

the boy in wet boots,
the green lane that winds
all among my roots.

The stick, the ice crack,
the hoof pocks, the ditch.
The brick heap, the track,

the ladder-sided cart;
old black orchards
branching through the heart.

The outback roads

Scrub on fire and a red road
smoking in its pendulum swing
pinned to a point. Arterial bleed
into air and dust, into the vast
ticking of time.
                        The quiet song
laying a line subtle as mist
I hear as a sunk river, a snake
of many heads passing to a pool
shared and known.
                        Blood red smoke
of roads straightening into a sun
that will stop all but the slow coil
of the old way from skin to skin.

NEVERLASTING

CLIMATE CHANGE is a reality; it is rapid and accelerating; it is snuffing the glaciers from the mountains, overwhelming our towns with tropical rains and drawing the sea in over the land. Snow no longer blankets the southern English hills, winter by winter. Arctic-alpine flowers are moving up the hillsides in Upper Teesdale, up the mountains in Scotland to where things are still cool enough for them. Cold weather birds are moving north, or staying there. Cold water fish are flocking north, and the seabirds of the lonely Atlantic rocks cannot cope with the disappearance of their food source.

The fish are also facing depletion, perhaps extinction, from over-fishing, from fish-catching technology that is too smart to let any of them escape. Hedges and lanes are quieter at dawn and in spring, meadows lie uniformly green and flower-free, cornfields an unbroken gold. Hares, hedgehogs, yellowhammers, snipe …

It would be just a sad old man's lament, typical of those cried by the old men of each generation for 10,000 years – if it were not for the evidence of my own eyes and ears as I go walking.

'THE GLACIER WEEPS' – Walking up from Hintertux at the head of the Zillertal in the Austrian Alps, I found the lower skirt of the glacier shrinking and shedding meltwater and clinkery rocks.

'SNOW ON CLOVER' – At the end of July 1832 William Cobbett set off from London to ride through Surrey, Sussex and Hampshire. On 30 July he passed through the countryside around Worth in north Sussex. In his great work of English travel and social commentary, *Rural Rides*, Cobbett's notes for that day record how the woods had been stunted by frosts and wintry winds that persisted until midsummer.

'THE INVADED' – Above Kirriemuir in Angus, driving up narrow Glen Clova towards high roadless hills, I felt an acute sense of my car-borne self as an agent of change.

'LAZARUS SWIM' – This poem was provoked by an image on the BBC News website of a huge heap of cod stacked on a trawler's deck before being thrown back dead into the sea – purely because the boat had exceeded its allotted quota of fish.

'FOR THE DROWNING' – A winter walk in the Cotswolds after unprecedented rainfall and floods had hit southern England in 2000.

'ANXIOUS SKY' – On the low-lying Suffolk coast in 2006 I walked one autumn evening along the tall and stout seawall from Walberswick to Dunwich, returning by paths through Dingle Marshes. The seawall barrier separated the freshwater marshes, a nature reserve famous for its bird life, from the sea. At first light next morning I went out to watch the birds, to find that the night's high tide had overtopped the seawall, torn it down, and flooded the marshes as far as the ancient Suffolk coastline half a mile inland.

'SEA BEATING' – Walking the sea wall of Canvey Island on the Essex shore of the Thames Estuary I got into conversation with an elderly man, and heard of the terrors of the night of 31 January/1 February 1953, when a North Sea surge burst the defences and flooded the island, drowning 58 people.

The glacier weeps

Old glass heart softens, melting
at long last. High above Hintertux
the glacier weeps, bowed down before
what the blind call beautiful:
the mad sun in all her anger,
baked blue of the pressure-cooker
lid settling over the world.
                         Summer,
the everlasting lord, peremptorily expels
gentians and snowy owls, refugees with
passports expired. There will be
salt graves for islanders, the old god
foreshadows; sundays for ever in the
new religion.
                         Out rush the springs,
green for what passes, black
for what comes in. The glacier mourns,
giving birth to stones as bare as bones.

Snow on clover

The woods have not shot much this year, says
Cobbett, frowning from horseback. The cold
winds, the frosts that we had up to
midsummer prevented the trees from growing much.
Frosts in June, you moan, cantankerous old
grumbler and rider who never dreamed of such
weathers as haunt us through these bluebell days
in January along the holloways.

Now that the worst of winters is over,
over for ever, give me the shiver
and the unshifting, the clamped and shining river
iced into spring, a glass tumbling
and the old radical grumbling
of frosted hazel shoots, of snow on clover.

The invaded

Coming up from the moor town
the long strath cradled all that
was left of the road, rocked it in green

arms of meadow, in a drumlin bed.
The river murmured to it, the larch groves
smoothed down the light and a curlew cried

upland vespers for the deadly thing.
They could not draw its sting, these allies,
with soft complaint and sweetness of song;

nor mine, herding them ever north
with my stick of good intention, footsoldier,
sower of salt and dragon teeth.

Lazarus swim

A flake of fire from McGregor's hard-lit
cigarette. One gasp: the thick
lips part as a hurt brother's might.
A fluff of ash on the glazed lake
of the iris, on the armoured coat.

Salt drops darken the rusty deck
under these starers. One bows its back,
snaps like a spring, gasping forth
life from the pursed string of a mouth,
subtle in its knots. Back to the dark

they will be shed, a Lazarus swim,
heads down, gliding still as stone
to the living bed they were rousted from
a cigarette ago. McGregor smokes on
stolidly: never a fanciful man.

For the drowning

Severn's out and into houses. Old
gods, nothing will satisfy their cold
hunger but ruin. Arun's about, and Adur.
Since October no moon seen,
the sun abolished. Bloodstained Wye has been
forcing tribute. Each walker's a wader,
a booted struggler among melting clods,
probing and stumbling under the sky's rods.

Wylye's up. The muscled silver back
bends to the work, harrowing green to black,
sowing the valley with self. Bristle-necked
willows suck till they choke; there's more
here than they can deal with. Brooks roar
at river strength, streamlets will have us wrecked.
Windrush, Misbourne: you are watched like sour
lovers, your moods weighed hour to hour

till you come bursting. Sandbags at the door
to keep Coln from firesides. I saw
Rack Isle steeped, Arlington Row beset;
heard, 'Never known it like this,' and glanced
up as I sloshed, to where boughs danced
howling. Perhaps we've seen nothing yet:
preliminaries. I shivered, picturing some frowning
arkbuilder judging who'll be for the drowning.

Anxious sky

We watched it from the hill at first light,
the sea eating the marsh. A man told
how he'd heard the bank go in the night,
seen the silver tide lift through, the cold

sense of it. I did not say
what tugged like a beak at my inner eye –
how from the marsh path yesterday
in a fretting wind, under an anxious sky,

I viewed a frantic dance
of gulls in freakish terror over the barrier
and had wondered at it, at what chance
orchestrator, what hawk or what harrier.

Sea beating

You should have seen that sea beating
into our house in the dark. The blow
that burst the door in, cold
slap of the wave in my father's face,
contemptuously.
                    Men had built below
the tides like arrogant lords in a fable,
trusting old Dutchmen's skill in
walling and dyking, their famous
know-how.
                    Upstairs we crouched
at the windows, watching the waves'
discipline, their soldierly regularity,
marching one by one through
the house, slapping and smashing, exacting
conqueror's rights.
                    Trust no experts,
as we trusted, but pack your things.
Quit the silty coast lands;
the sea has its eye on them.
Keep watch from higher ground. If you had
seen that tide beating into
our house, you would not sleep easy
behind sea walls.

DEVIL COMING

I CAN'T ESCAPE the news. It comes at me from all quarters. What reached my forefathers diluted by time, ignorance and distance hits me full on as soon as it has happened – or long beforehand, in the form of ominous speculation that ups the ante all the time. And this immediate nature of TV and internet reportage, the vivid images and block capital style, lend the news an urgency and portent that suck me in and make me feel personally involved, however far-flung the topic, whether I like it or not.

'BY THE WATERS OF PONTCHARTRAIN' – New Orleans, August 2005: The image of the Superdome crammed with 25,000 downtown refugees, islanded in unspeakable conditions in the floodwaters of Hurricane Katrina, took up residence in my mind and could not be shifted.

'THE COCKLERS' – Crossing the vast tidal plain of Morecambe Bay on foot, you learn of its treacherous quicksands and deceptive tide flows from the Sands Guide, Cedric Robinson, as he shepherds you safely across. The 23 Chinese cockle pickers drowned there in the dark on 5 February 2004 were trapped as much by their own poverty, their illegal presence in the country and the ruthless greed of the people-smugglers and gang organisers who abandoned them here as by the rising tide.

'PHISSAIEE' – The onomatopoeic Greek word for the blowing of a mighty wind. The NATO bombing of Serbia took place in the spring of 1999 while I was walking through Crete. I was carrying the Psalms with me for inspiration, reading three a day, and happened to have reached the violent and apocalyptic Psalm 18 on the day that a fierce hot wind from Africa blew in across the island. In the mountain village of Kritsa the old men had taken refuge from the wind in the kafenion, where the TV was relaying horrific and very graphic images of civilian casualties incurred during a NATO bombing raid on Belgrade. Somehow all this came together in the poem.

By the waters of Pontchartrain

By the waters of Pontchartrain
they sit down and weep and cry on
their brothers, but all in vain.

They plead for water and bread, the bare staff
of life snatched up by a winnowing
blowing them out as chaff.

There in the round house among the waters
the old man with the mojo hand
deals with their sons and daughters.

High on soft airs, from blue skies
we glance below. Tilting white wings,
calmly we balance, easily rise.

She is not spent, the goddess grown
terrible on the face of the waters.
From her bowl of chaos she has sown

with the hand of a harvest-giver
strange fruit in the trees, shadowed
movements in lake and river.

Read here a whole bible of sorrow:
a stormed city, an outcast people
rising on a furious tomorrow.

The cocklers

Then they heard it: the foam
bearded devil coming for them
through the banks. Godwits and terns
wailing and shrieking before him.
Shrouded in wet hessian, the
fishjaw crunch of ribbed
shells. Coats swam into the
tides, rubber boots bobbed.

Tears blow through Fujian province,
salty as estuary winds
and as negligible. Here's
the real deal: the slippery sounds
of rib-edged coins creeping
from palm to palm, like tides through sands.

Phissaiee: the great wind

'... and he rode upon a cherub, and did fly; yea he did fly upon the wings of the wind.' (Psalm 18)

The cat fussed her kitten under my chair
this morning, licking it, yowling uneasily, though
all seemed well. Stormcrow in black, the old

woman came, wrapped to the eyes, fluttering:
bad news in black rags. The day
thickened, darkened. Then *phissaiee*

roared down on Kritsa; hot blast
pouring east from Africa over the town,
a prophet shriek out of the desert, raging.

Groves thrashed; green seas of leaves
hissed like cats, turning white eyes to heaven.
Dark dots flew, men or birds, storm-driven.

Doors clashed, chairs scattered, tempers
grated like sand. Old men growled, watching
war on the screen, Balkan neighbours burn.

'Thunder in the heavens,' cried the prophet,
'lightnings, hail stones and coals of fire.'
Apocalyptic, as from a frescoed church,

these breaths of hell: sliced men, babies
cooked and smoking, mothers in flames. Kritsa
crouched, back to the wall; *phissaiee*

scourged eyes to tears. 'Then did I beat them
small as the dust before the wind,' the prophet
foamed, 'I cast them out, as dirt in the streets.'

All day the cat prowled, circling
the chair where I skulked, one of the
ungodly, bowed under a blast from heaven.

CROSSING THE SOUND

Poems spring from a number of mostly unfathomable sources. I am sometimes tempted to refrain from visiting one or another of these internal wells because I do not want to recognise, or would like to avoid, the reflection that I see there. For example, the cast of many of my poems seems dark. Many betray a preoccupation with death. I don't know why. I don't see myself consciously in that light. But this sombre source is one that never seems to runs dry.

'DEAD MAN'S STITCH' – In Nelson's Navy, those sewing casualties of battle into their hammocks for sea burial would plant a 'dead man's stitch' between the eyes of the victim to avert the possibility of a mistake. If the sailor were by any chance still alive, tears would automatically well from the eyes in response to the needle's prick.

'THE BROTHERS' – In honour of Conchubhar O'Driscoll, ferry skipper of Cape Clear Island in Roaringwater Bay, Co Cork

'THE LONG STREET' – In appreciation of Rodney Whitaker, writer and conversationalist at Dinder in Somerset

'THE MINER' and 'INSIDE THE HIDE' – Inner workings.

'FOR THE MAN GONE' – My dear friend, musician and life enhancer, Dave Pinney of Somerset

'THE MARGARET ROBIN' – In memory of Margaret Walford of Bredon Hill

'THE GREAT TREE IS TAKEN DOWN' – Alan Woolley, doctor and gardener, PoW 1940–5.

Dead man's stitch

They tamed the preacher with a scourge
he plaited himself under the bo'sun's
grin, braiding his pressed man's pain
over, under and through the surge
of self broken small on duty:
the futile self, beating in vain
against the breakers.

                So he owned
a plainer God, cursing him down
in yardarm dramas on black
ice-rink nights. Wind honed,
storm tempered, rope calloused;
self battened deep, slack
taken up hard.

                Now he's stretched
stiff in the scuppers. The needle sews
canvas to flesh: dead man's stitch
between the eyes that must have fetched
tears from warm ducts, had not his passion
drained all cold. So they ditch
the empty shell.

                There he glides,
the glinting hammock man, where sharks
snatch at his bubble halo. The blind
sea accepts a tear that slides
out of the dead man's stitch as salt
to salt, one drop to melt the rind
of God's deep mind.

The brothers

You have taken the stony lane to the
landing stage, to your brother's small
table and his weighing hut. A toddy
to oust the cold, and now the coin spins
between you, only for luck; he will
carry a brother of the guild for joy
of crossing the sound with you in his
dark boat bowed like a dolphin.

There will be a continuous darting of boats
passing and repassing among the shoals
of Roaringwater, a march of gleams and
rainshadows, of shadows lifting from lanes
and seaways, and a dolphin seen
glinting between the rocks and the ferry.

The long street

Above the road float the lighted
squares of the window. They show
a calm face to night and the
shape in the yellow lamp glow.

We will go in at
the white gate and crunch the gravel
and climb the stair to the wizard's
lair, and there will ravel and unravel.

At the chairside we unload him
cargo that holds smells of rain,
tangs of cattle and horses and
a tug of wind along a damp lane.

We clash the rusty claymores of
our wits with cool steel;
we cross grains, we hit and
are hit, we trade smacks and smile

over the bale we unbind,
Rapunzel-like. We taste the flood
of a wry sight and a crowded mind,
and of life that beats on in the blood,

pulse to pulse against that
pale unwanted guest,
beats for the cagebird
fluttering at the bars of the breast,

and a heart that breathes
how on aerial feet
he has leaped the hedges, has
hurdled the brook and run the long street.

The miner

He hears you now; tireless
hewer in his workings.
Out of the deep where you

work, up from the bud
and the bloom. The body
you hollow, the tunnel, the trap,

the tap, tap of your pick.
Ever the winner, jealous
cutter of songs, of wings.

Rush up bricks, baulks,
into the breach. Cradle his
breath. Block death.

Inside the hide

Death has entered her, spun her high,
and laid her by, quite gently. She lies
hunched into the verge: a curved badger,
healthy-looking, the colour of old snow.

Whatever catastrophic breakage such an
end implies is not on show. The smooth
fur looks strokeable. No red squash of
guts; she has been spared the pillory,

public humiliation, the flat thin
grin smeared from here to there for flies
to rub their hands over. Her shape
retains dignity, a quiet privacy.

Two sides to it. One, the soft
exterior thump, out in the night, so modest
as hardly to jar the wheel, one blink
splitting the dry glare of concentration,

instantly dismissed. Its corollary:
branched tubes of veins terribly lit,
brilliantly; no sooner lit than burst
onto an inner eyelid's wintry canvas,

twinned with the unimaginable blow.
Cubs in the sett, genes in the hoarded sperm
wasted inside the hide. Here's ruin so complete
that death's ashamed to put it on display.

For the man gone

We thought of the man gone, the laugh crafter;
of tall tales and of tunes and of the boots,
the ridiculous boots of his dancing, the hoots
and the spilling of tunes and of kindnesses, the taking of hands in
    need
and a soul crouched like a seed.

The man gone – is he over and done, all that brave
hooray thrown away?

We must love unbridled,
must ride life like a ribboned skiff, a fiery comet
of tails, with music and pandemonium in our sails
and a bright wake of light to scatter
like seeds, let fall as seeds of spice into flavourless clay.

So we will break night, and out of it
we will rescue day.

The Margaret robin

He carries you carefully out of the church
between his large young hands, this grandson whom
you have carried, carefully, in work-worn hands.

Strange to think of so much spirit, wide and
green as a garden, caught in so small a
polished wood casket, if it were caught there

and not, as we are beginning to feel, freed
and helping to spread over all the black
hats and grey heads this extraordinary blue day.

Out of the ashes no enamelled phoenix in
basilisk pride, but a bird such as you were, a
red-flush restless robin with quick eyes

sharp to see what needs to be done about
whom, a keen beak open to urge,
chat, chide, point upwards to what's light

and green, as someone knowing. We'll look for you in
your Bredon garden, and all gardens. Changing your
dress to suit the seasons – January robin, May wren – you'll

dart through us; seen or sensed in how
things grow, fruit, fall, seed; heard
on breezes off the hill, multiplied, joyful.

The great tree is taken down

The great tree is taken down
at last. The rooted oak that stood to the
scream and the blast

lies in the shackles. Great tree
split apart, the wedge in the dark
driven to the heart

of ninety rings. Count each out: nor deep
nor shallow but takes its stain from five
of bitter fallow,

yet of rich bloom; long fruiting
into light, a guardian at the gate of
many men's night.

There are more trees, more trees in
this wood. They tremble at the hollow where
the great tree stood.

HEARING VOICES

THE VOICE OF THE PAST, sometimes in harmony with, sometimes contesting with that of the present, heard in groves and catacombs, foreign lands, close at home, in a graveyard of boats, on a quiet breath in the back of the imagination.

'GOD'S TRICK' – Written after visiting the venerable yews of Kingley Vale in West Sussex.

'DEAD BOATS' – A clutch of superannuated fishing boats lie rotting in a mud-choked dock at King's Lynn where the Great Ouse meets the Wash.

'FEGYVERBE!' – Public statues from Hungary's Communist era, toppled from their pedestals around Budapest during the fall of the dictatorship in 1989, have been exiled to Statue Park beyond the borders of the city. 'Fegyverbe!' means 'To Arms!'

'ETRUSCAN MESSAGES' – Everyone has heard of the Romans, but who knows of their forerunners the Etruscans? In northern Italy, in the lands between the Arno and the Tiber, the Etruscans developed a colourful, life-loving, deeply spiritual and sensual civilization between 800 and 300 BC, before the Romans moved in to crush and subdue them. Their dead were laid to rest in stone sarcophagi, their own effigies lying above them on the coffin lids, each recumbent statue propped up on one elbow and staring intently towards the doorway of the tomb. Underground in the painted tombs of the Tarquinia necropolis, vivid frescoes show the Etruscans in all their vigour and liveliness – courting, feasting, hunting birds and deer, making love, making merry in the woods and fields of Lazio, celebrating the pleasures of life at the very gates of the Underworld.

'UNKNOWING' – Arab Saracens invaded Crete in AD 824 and ruled the island for the next 137 years. The story of their rule in Crete remains virtually unknown. In 961 the Byzantine general Nikephoros Phokas took their capital Rabdh-el-Khandak after a siege which involved catapulting the heads of his captives into the city. The Saracens were expelled from Crete, leaving behind them almost nothing except stark rumours of barbarism.

This poem was written before the events of 11 September 2001.

'ICE HOLE' – Watching a TV programme about our Ice Age ancestors, it struck me that they were at least as far removed in time from the builders of the great Stone Age tombs of Europe as those builders are from us.

God's trick

When a yew grows old, I have read –
and some, like branched longstones, stood
eight thousand years worshipped in the wood –
it splits to let the wind blow rot
and rain through, unblocked. Having shed
carapace, the heart melts. It is not
for the yew to tease out reasons
for its death after forty thousand seasons,

but to be green and grow. Hence the shoot
that the dying core feeds, the great need
of each cell for the next; to root
out of the rot, to set millennial seed.
This is God's trick, of being new
yet old. No wonder men venerate the yew.

Dead boats

The dock keeps them from you like a shore girl's
arms; deep, hollowed, a soft bed
locking them in, gently shrouding each
shrunken strake with fronds. The warm mud

cradles, mummifies. Unprepared for
deeds or death, *Baden Powell* lies
all but buried. Have you forgotten them,
salty river, who tracked your ways

in Boston Deeps, nosed your channels, scooped
your secret pools? *Kenneth William* splits
dry sides; pale timbers shiver; spartina grass
tickles the joyless ribs. *Captain Oates*

sinks in the bricked-off dock. Don't you want them,
Great Ouse, you rough vibrant muscle of tide,
sinewy arm of the sea bent round
the waist of Lynn, pumping with life, with blood

of rivers' flood? Burst the dock, then;
suck all out, gorge on the dead boats –
organic resurrection of spent names
and bones of ghosts feeding your silty roots.

Fegyverbe!

'Fegyverbe! To arms!' you yell, giant
worker-warrior, stuck in your one vast
stride. Around you in the frozen silence
of Statue Park, workers and soldiers reach
for a sky gridded black with cables.
Orators wave their proletarian caps,
bronze arms rise against a sea of
troubled cloud scudding in from the west.

Behind your children's backs and their shrugged
shoulders, brandishing a black flag and
a righteous heart forged in a red
foundry where your heirs will never labour,
'Fegyverbe! Fegyverbe!' you are still roaring,
glaring portentously back into Buda.

Etruscan messages

Laris Partunus raises his right hand,
perhaps in blessing. We have ordained him a sober
priest of the Etruscans, bearded stranger
on a sarcophagus lid. His putative son
Velthur Partunus sleeps alongside, a horned
river god under his feet. 'Magnate'
we style him. 'Il Obeso, Fatty'
is how we rationalize the sag of lardy
breasts, the jelly belly of Laris Velthurson
the grandson beyond. We do not know
their good, their bad, their ugly. But we have
their names in stone, a deceiving intimacy.

Under the pale Tarquinian ploughlands we wrest
messages from grave paintings, gleanings of
revelation from these nobles who may have been
rogues, thieves, lechers, unlettered scum
of the tomb-rich earth. Laris and Velthur Partunus;
we read their truths like tablets of stone:

> *hungry lions hunt the deer,*
> *winners bully losers,*
> *drinking rotgut makes you queer,*
> *young girls scorn old boozers,*
> *poor men work until they die,*
> *rich men spend their money,*
> *love is sweet but makes you sigh,*
> *sex is dark and funny.*

Unknowing

Shadowy, those Saracens, bequeathing
scarce footprints, light but cruel;
curved swords loosed from ships,
eagle noses savouring fresh blood,
scorched rafters.
                           Why did they not
build, paint, sculpt in marble?
Pain and destruction: could these have sustained
a century of gold-ringed nobles?

Basilicas toppled, towns melted, a thousand
private or public Golgothas. Sum total
a blank; negative time.
                           Then this
grotesque curtain call, the sky over Khandakas
raining heads. Clipped beards catapulted,
eagle beaks broken on Byzantine stone;
what the modern mind grasps, barbarism
dealt to barbarians.
                           Expunged, a slate
wiped clean. Folk devils fallen
out of retrieval into that desert of
dry dusty hearts we allot them,
unseeing, unknowing.

Ice hole

Into the axe-broken hole they slide you,
through dark discs of water
already glazing with a new skin.

The woman cries;
it was her sealbone needle pursing the stiff
lips of the reindeer shroud that caught
a flash of cold sun this dawn.
Winter enters the hole of her heart.

Far in the future there will be
obsequies in great halls of the dead
for such as you; brave whorls of
sun graven in the stones for you,
and a task, a breath of life to pass
back from over the world's edge.

For now there is nothing but a black eye closing
in the white face of the lake.

A tusk stroke did for you in the late
afternoon, in the ring of men and dogs.
It was not the bayed beast's
strength that smacked you flat in the snow, but
weakness, a crack in
a stone blade unchecked.

Tears freeze on the woman's
blue-patterned cheeks. She howls,
grasping her belly in widespread
fingers of fur.
               Your sons,
should they survive the grief and the
wolf unseen among the birch trunks and
whatever winters may bring,
will hear word of your mistakes.

Blades will grow stronger, minds sharpen
beyond flint and chert.

Fabulous halls of the dead,
fit for godlike builders,
one day will rise beyond the snowfields in some
now undreamable time of songs and sunny grazing.

APART TOGETHER

Travel in all its aspects begins and ends with people. It is the chance strangers I have met and will never meet again, the friends I have made all over the world who have accompanied me to the peaks and depths, who make the bedrock and backbone of all countries and landscapes, and every city and wild place.

'HOW ISLANDS WEATHER STORMS' – Travelling through the remote North Sea archipelago of the Faroe Islands, my host on Borðoy island was Asbjørn Lomaklett, headmaster of Klaksvik school, a man very steadily balanced between following the traditional Faroese way of life and that of a 21st-century person. He told me of how he had been approached by the little daughter of one of his ex-pupils, a trawler skipper who had just been killed at sea.

'BLOOD BROTHERS' and 'THE WHISTLER' – Two Cretan moments.

'GOGGIN'S TUNE' – Late for a meeting and in a hurry, I was nevertheless transported by this encounter.

'CURMUDGEON MAN' – Growing older, but far from gracefully.

'THE CLIMB AND THE DARK CLOUD' – In memory of my father, John Somerville, a lifelong hill walker.

'SHAPING' – Among friends in the Taverna Aravanes on a starry night in the Amari Valley, a glass of wine on the table with a slice of apple in it 'to sweeten the talk', Neonakis the sculptor playing the laouto, Lambros singing with his right arm thrown high, and out across the valley the dogs of seven villages barking down the moon.

How islands weather storms

'Asbjørn' – a timid playground voice –
'will you be my father now?'
– and you see the wave falling,
blood on the wheelhouse glass, raw
hearts in a red-roofed house on the blue
icy shine of Haraldssund.

'Asbjørn-father ... ' Can you bear that,
teacher of fathers? A blade of wind
slides up the fjord. The heart
turns over. Her small cold hand
closes like a link. Your mind
cannot dredge up the bearded skipper;

it is a fair-haired Klaksvik boy
who rises, one of ten thousand. His eyes
appeal through hers. You have trodden
the same track, the Faroese
dance that is chain and embrace,
bind and weave. Out on Kalsoy

you and he have chased sheep,
snared puffins, hung hay to dry,
meat for salt wind to cure;
have beached your boats, entered the grey
hides of whales and the cutting joy
of blood frenzy on a soaked

strand in a red stew of wavelets.
Gently-spoken Asbjørn, shall a father
give a hungry child a stone?
You nod and sigh, taking another
craft in tow: how islands weather
storms, shoulder winters together.

Blood brothers

The old man sits, and I sit: I
head on hand, tired from the road; he
chin on crook, bent with work. Serrated
leaves of an aspen shade us equally,

both sleepy, both blue-trousered. No
other point of contact I can see,
except this fly that blends the old man's blood
and mine together, democratically.

The whistler

Stealing through the ruined village,
alert for ghosts or straying dogs,
I paused. Among the tumbled walls
someone was whistling, sweet and low.

'Hello?' I called. 'Hello?' It sheared
the tune off sharp. Nobody moved,
came or called back. We waited. Insects
ticked. The hot walls baked. At last

I tiptoed on, and heard the whistler
pick up the tune, hesitantly,
not so sweetly: the sound of someone
alert for ghostly footfalls.

Goggin's tune

It was the tinny wheeze of the
mouth organ stopped me on
Oxford Street, a cold night.

A wintry head ducked low,
a mouth cupped by two old hands
into shadow; a rusty arpeggio

repeated and repeated. Goggin,
he said, Joe Goggin. He spelt
the name out: Goggin, a Corkman.

We invoked the Buttermarket
above in Shandon under the bells
unheard by him in forty years,

and nearer the river, Beamish's
brewery. Yes, he'd known that –
too well, maybe, he shrugged.

I threw a pound into the empty
cap, asked for 'Skibbereen Lasses'.
He shook his head against the roar:

I don't do them old tunes,
folks can't hear 'em for the traffic.
I guessed he couldn't really play.

All evening the Corkman's
rusty anti-tune dogged me down,
pricking and needling under the skin,

raising the ghosts of old ones –
'The Boys of Schull', 'Ballydehob' –
lighting the night lanes of London,

shading in the green islands,
whales in Roaringwater Bay
and the blue salty face of day.

Curmudgeon Man

I lump myself up, poke my elbows
out like a spiked bush, scowl like a
bad old bear.

Sandwich munchers, lovers enwrapped, mobile
chatterers, keyboard clickers all can read:
sit well clear.

I will impose my whim, I will force
hesitaters, seatside ditherers
to look elsewhere.

This railway ogre – how long has he
been swelling under my skin, covertly
grumbling for air?

Soon it will not be trains alone that wake
Curmudgeon Man, seldom to cede an inch,
never to share.

Clip back those thorns, I warn myself;
draw in those claws, you ageing fool:
have a care.

Save your breath, myself growls back: this is
my own self-excavated lair. No-one
will touch me here.

The climb and the dark cloud

It is the young climbers who fall beyond
their futures. What of the old men?
I had a father, a Sisyphus who fought
his burden continually to the peaks. He caught
snatches there, could glimpse the bridge; then
the downfall of stones, the slough of despond.
Embattled trudger that I loved, bowed
to the climb and the dark cloud.

I found a snapshot after he went –
a man of my age, smiling wide,
jokes on his lips. No black wings
crooked in the shadows behind the look of things;
no sack of stones? Nothing to bear, to hide?
Well, I will go and ask him in the bent
grass of the mountain, along the cloudy ridge
that brings us to the chasm and the bridge.

Shaping

Neonakis, your leonine eyes
have seen it all, or most of it.
Now they stare down at the
scurry of your thick sculptor's fingers.

Out in the valley the night
takes shape under great Psiloritis;
stars crowding over Thronos, and
stars fallen in heaps in other villages:
lights on sloping streets grown beautiful
with distance, and the hoarse voices of dogs.

From an olive-wood fretboard polished
by earthy fingertips, you
raise the light heart of Theodorakis,
as you shape a strong man from a stone.

Andonis is here, tired from
the orange earth of his vineyard;
Costas, and Nikos the teaser, and the palikari
George with one hand tight on the
throat of his devil, and a mantinade
shaping in his own dry throat;

and Lambros, rapping a wine glass
on the table to our health and to the
windy night and singing dogs and the moon
dancing on the pale horns of Psiloritis.

Dance on, the sculptor's fingers; I will put
the bad old guitar across my knee and join this
making and shaping out of olive stones and
oil stains, stories and fragments of tunes.

CHRISTOPHER SOMERVILLE is a writer, journalist, presenter and the author of more than 30 books. He has written extensively on travel for the *Daily Telegraph* and other national newspapers over some 20 years, and specialises in exploring out-of-the-way places on foot, particularly in the British Isles – journeys reflected in these poems.

His first collection of poems, *Extraordinary Flight,* was published by Rockingham Press in 2000, and in 2007 his *The Golden Step: A Walk through the Heart of Crete* was published in Haus Publishing's 'Armchair Traveller' series.